Private Equity Backed Succession Buyouts

European University Studies

Europäische Hochschulschriften
Publications Universitaires Européennes

Series V
Economics and Management

Reihe V Série V
Volks- und Betriebswirtschaft
Sciences économiques, gestion d'entreprise

Vol./Bd. 3356

PETER LANG
Frankfurt am Main · Berlin · Bern · Bruxelles · New York · Oxford · Wien

Maxim David Littek

Private Equity Backed Succession Buyouts

Explorative Study of Critical Success Factors

PETER LANG
Internationaler Verlag der Wissenschaften

Bibliographic Information published by the Deutsche Nationalbibliothek
The Deutsche Nationalbibliothek lists this publication in the Deutsche Nationalbibliografie; detailed bibliographic data is available in the internet at http://dnb.d-nb.de.

ISSN 0531-7339
ISBN 978-3-631-60003-0

www.peterlang.de

Preface

Family businesses rightly are considered to be the backbone of the German economy. Sooner or later most of these businesses are confronted with a change of ownership, largely due to the retirement of the generation running the business. The issue of succession, whether transferring business assets from one generation to another or divesting to third parties, not only poses a considerable challenge for affected businesses, but also for the economy at large.

Private equity investors offer one solution for family businesses facing succession by actively investing in these businesses through the managed process of a buyout or buyin. Not seldom, however, the process is impeded by misinformation or distrust among the parties involved. The author developed his interest in this largely unexplored field of research into a dissertation on private equity backed succession buyouts. The presented work includes the insights of numerous interview partners as well as first-hand knowledge from the author's practical experience in the private equity market. An unabridged version of the presented work was submitted as a doctoral dissertation in November 2008.

In the meantime the 2008/2009 financial market crisis brought dramatic change to the world economy and put international private equity markets abruptly under pressure. Taking into account difficulties in acquiring both equity and debt financing in the current economic environment, the author acknowledges that the strength of individual factors impacting on the realization of private equity backed succession buyouts might have changed. Nevertheless, it must be assumed that the profound shifting of the economy only is of temporary nature and that financial markets - including the market for private equity financings - continue to recover to full stability in due course.

In any case, it continues to be necessary to find solutions to the succession issue in medium-sized German family businesses. For this reason in particular the author remains confident about the value of the study's findings.

Maxim David Littek
Berlin, November 2009

Acknowledgements

Forewords generally are read before a research study although written after. This is reasonable since by this means the reader is able to learn who contributed to the origination of the henceforth completed study. At this point it is the author's wish to thank everyone that supported the long evolution of this study.

At the heart of this research are the statements and reports of family business owners, institutional private equity investors, managers with buyout experience and experts with a professional background in consultancy. Without the generous support of these interview partners the present study would not have been possible. For that reason the author is much indebted to the study's participants and is thankful for their openness, invaluable insights and trust they have put in the author.

The author is also indebted to Prof. Dr. Dr. Jozef Komornik who allocated the necessary freedom to deal with the topic in the presented form. His suggestions, encouragement and corrections made a valuable contribution to the success of this research project. Sincere thanks also appertain to Prof. Dr. Ottmar Schneck for his continual guidance and support throughout this study.

From the initial conception of the research question to the press date of this book many steps were necessary during which I repeatedly experienced the extraordinary endorsement of my family and friends. To them my special gratitude appertains.

Maxim David Littek

Acknowledgements

Contents

1 Introduction

Chapter one builds the introduction to this research study. This chapter outlines the study's research context (chapter 1.1), the research objective (chapter 1.2) and the state of research in the field (chapter 1.3).

1.1 Research context

Family businesses are often described to be the backbone of the German economy. Without doubt they assume a prominent role in Germany's business landscape. According to the Institut für Mittelstandsforschung (IfM) Bonn, in access of 95 percent of all German businesses exhibit characteristics typical of family businesses; these businesses provide 57 percent of all employment relationships and contribute 42 percent of aggregate turnover in Germany (IfM Bonn 2007a: 24). Next to this economic denotation, family businesses typically exhibit distinct characteristics such as value based business policies and a concurrent commitment to tradition and innovation. In this regard they assume a considerable socio-political role in German society as well.

At the same time, approximately 70,900 German family businesses are confronted with succession every year, thereby affecting around ten times as many employment relationships in these businesses. Every year on average 6,000 German family businesses discontinue operations due to unresolved succession (IfM Bonn 2007b). Surprisingly, despite the inevitability of succession, few family businesses prepare for succession in advance and many do not undergo any formal succession planning at all (EVCA 2005: 10 et sq.).

A succession problem might arise when continuity of leadership is jeopardized due to retirement, retreat for other reasons or sudden demise of the family business owner. Although succession within the family is typically the premier choice of family business owners, only in less than half of all cases succession within the family is realized (IfM Bonn 2007b). Foremost, this circumstance must be attributed to the lack of sufficiently qualified or interested successor candidates within the family and/or the conflicts that arise when more than one suitable family candidate is available.

The organization of leadership continuity at the topmost business level is a central problem for medium-sized family businesses and obviously an essential precondition for business perpetuation. In cases of neglect and unsatisfactory solutions the advantages of structures in medium-sized family businesses might be damaged or lost, leading to a degradation of efficiency and situations of crisis. In that way often exclusively those businesses with a discontinuance of leadership, that have been very successful previously, fall into crisis-like situations with subsequent insolvency (Albach/Freund 1989: 22).

A private equity backed succession constitutes one solution to the succession problem. Here, institutional private equity investors actively invest in businesses seeking succession through the managed process of a buyout (MBO) or buyin (MBI).[1] In difference to a divestment of the family business to strategic investors that are oftentimes exclusively interested in synergy effects or individual assets, a divestment to an entrepreneurial management team backed by a private equity investment company allows for the perpetuation of the targeted business as an independent entity. Further, a buyout ideally combines elements of trust with the vendor's intention to safeguard the business's identity. Family businesses thereby have the opportunity to remain independent, relationships to clients and suppliers might be preserved and the business philosophy perpetuated (Wright/Coyne 1985: 11 et sq., Thomson 1988: 5 et sq., Luippold 1991: 22). Such non-monetary concerns of family business owners - which are typically jeopardized in case of a divestment to industrial investors - might even make a private equity backed buyout attractive to family business owners albeit lower sales proceeds are attainable.

Since 2001 the buyout segment has evolved to be the most intensive investment segment not only in Germany but also in other European private equity markets. The total reported buyout volume in Germany in 2006 amounts to EUR 2.6 billion. That accounts for more than 2/3 (72 percent) of all reported private equity investment (including venture capital) in Germany in 2006 (BVK 2007b: 2). Despite the ample availability of both private equity and suitable investment opportunities, only few family business owners in Germany opt for a buyout solution to the succession problem. Although out of 2,600 German family businesses with more than 200 employees surveyed in 2005, 428 businesses (17 percent) considered to realize succession via a MBO and 780 (30 percent) considered succession in form of a MBI (IfM Bonn 2005), the percentages of actually realized MBO/MBI transactions are much lower. The IfM Bonn estimated that between 2005 and 2009 only 10 percent of German family businesses will realize

1 Subsequently, the term "buyout" will be used as a general term comprising of both "management buyout" *and* "management buyin" including hybrid forms unless otherwise stated; it is further assumed that all buyout transactions make use of considerable leverage. For an explicit discussion and confinement refer to chapter 2.3.3.

succession via a MBO and 17 percent by means of a MBI (IfM Bonn 2007b).[2] The question arises why this proportion remains relatively small, in particular in view of the ubiquity of the succession problem, frequently resulting in the discontinuation of family businesses. This question builds a central theme in the presented study.

The success and failure of succession in family businesses clearly has far-reaching implications for the economy at large. At the same time, private equity investment companies are ideally suited to accompany non-family succession routes such as MBOs and MBIs in medium-sized family businesses. The author therefore assumes that private equity investment companies are able to contribute to the perpetuation of the German "Mittelstand" and have a positive effect on the German economy.

1.2 Research objective

The preceding section highlighted the scope and relevancy of succession in family businesses and the need for an in-depth study of private equity backed succession buyouts as one potentially neglected succession alternative in family businesses.

From a *theoretical* point of view, the following deficiencies and limitations concerning the research field show the need for studying succession buyouts backed by institutional private equity investors. First, past research in the field has focused extensively on the technical aspects of buyout processes in both family and non-family businesses. However, since succession (i.e. ownership change) constitutes one of the most obvious investment rationales for private equity investors, it is surprising that this investment occasion has not been adequately researched to date. Second, most research on buyouts and succession in family businesses is deductive, hypothesis testing research relying on standardized (statistical) procedures or other means of quantification. This one-sided view reveals the need for inductive empirical projects and qualitative research designs. Third, research in the field is challenged to establish uniformity in defining suc-

2 Unfortunately, the IfM Bonn does not provide data on the percentage of MBOs and MBIs backed by institutional private equity. However, the author assumes that a considerable number - especially among larger transactions - is sponsored by institutional private equity investors (cp. chapter 2.2.3.2). In Forst's study for example, almost 95 percent of surveyed family businesses subject to a MBO/MBI received institutional private equity (Forst 1992: 55).

cess in succession. Thus, future research should reinforce efforts to gain consensus in questions of what dimensions of success are operationalizable.

From a *practical/empirical* perspective, studying succession scenarios outside the family is equally important since family business owners are still faced with contradictory research results and conflicting recommendations pertaining to non-family succession. First, a great amount of published research has aimed for rather universal research approaches that are neither country specific nor focus exclusively on private equity investments in context of family business succession. Second, previous research to a large extend is characterized by a preponderance of tax- and legal specific research foci on succession. Third, previous research is concerned with only broadly defined dimensions of success in family business succession or merely business survival and failure. The phenomenon of factors conducive to the closing of a private equity backed succession buyout transaction is almost unexplored. Finally, past research has not made use of such a broad base of empirical data employed in this study including data from all principally involved parties in private equity backed succession buyouts.

From these considerations emerges the focus of the study. Thereby it is essential to differentiate succession buyouts in German family businesses backed by institutional private equity investors from succession buyouts not involving institutional private equity. Equally it is of central importance to differentiate family businesses from non-family businesses. Further the focus is on German family businesses dissociating from businesses in other jurisdictions.

Surprisingly no grounding theory, not even a reliable data base for this group of businesses exists. This might be attributable to the ambiguity of the term "family business". A term not clearly defined is difficult to operationalize. One reason of practical importance is certainly that family businesses tend to be restrictive in publishing (financial) data. Often family businesses choose special structures of holding- and subsidiary enterprises only to reduce transparency for outsiders. On the other side family businesses lack an appropriate lobby; their appearance in academia and politics in relation to their economic relevance is benign. For this reason, both family business owners and potential successors lack fundamental knowledge which would help to prepare for challenges and opportunities specific to succession in family businesses.

Different authors researching reasons for the underdevelopment of private equity and venture capital markets in Germany have blamed the supply side (Kaufmann/Kokalj 1996: 14-20; Albach/Köster 1997: 17-23) just as much as the demand side (Plagge 2006: 96, Hack 2005: 1). Surprisingly, to date research concerned with private equity investments in Germany has not focused on private equity backed succession buyouts. To some degree this might be attributable to the fact that the access to family businesses and institutional private equity investors is equally difficult. Considering the increasing acceptance of private equity as an alternative source of equity financing for German (family) businesses it appears needful to source empirical insights specific to private equity backed succession buyouts.

Assuming that a medium-sized family business is free to choose among different succession alternatives, the author aims to pinpoint factors conducive to a buyout succession scenario backed by institutional private equity. The study differentiates between successful and non-successful cases of private equity backed succession buyouts in an attempt to delineate critical success factors (cp. Bullen 1981). Considering that agendas of principally involved parties differ considerably, the author opted to search for common ground objectives of the parties involved. Since the closing of the transaction typically constitutes the completion of ownership transfer and thus completion of the key aspect of succession and, on top, appears to be an integrative objective of all parties principally involved in the transaction, success in this study is exclusively constituted by the closing of the aforementioned transaction.

This study approaches the identified research needs by addressing the following central research question:

What are the individual contributions of factors underlying the private equity backed succession buyout process and its success?

The exploration of this research question follows the specifications of Kern's interaction theory (cp. Kern 1990) and focuses the analysis on (a) the *involved parties*, (b) the *framework conditions* and (c) the *transaction process* as three constitutive dimensions of factors decisively influencing the closure of private equity backed succession processes. Kern's theory thereby proved to be a suitable fundament for the structuring of empirical data ascertainment and the dissociation of individual success factors for analytic purposes. While the author assumes that many success factors are subject to control, other uncontrollable factors (such as factors related to or implicated by the external environment) potentially predetermine success and failure of private equity backed succession. Finally, objective of the study is a consistent frame of analysis that combines findings in the literature, normative deduction and empirical validation for the issue at hand.

Findings of the study should open up new ground in family business research and should build a foundation for future research addressing succession alternatives involving institutional private equity. The study's findings should have direct practical value in allowing family business owners, institutional private equity investors, managers seeking buyout opportunities and external consultants to (a) better understand each other's needs, (b) prepare for and organize private equity backed succession buyouts more effectively and (c) benefit directly from an objectification and holistic presentation of the issue at hand. In this sense the study's findings also aim to provide practitioners with knowledge elevating rational decision-making prior and during a private equity backed succession buyout. However, the study is not able to offer universal sample solutions. With respect to the particularities of individual circumstances each private equity backed succession buyout necessarily must be assessed on a stand-alone basis and offer custom made solutions.

1.3 State of Research

It can be acknowledged that the body of family business research has grown considerably over recent years. Nevertheless, family businesses continue to receive less attention by academia than corporate-type organizations and publicly listed businesses (cp. Klein 2000: 2). Further, although the literature on business formation is steadily increasing, the abandonment of entrepreneurial activity in context of succession has received comparatively little attention by researchers (cp. Bergamin 1995: 23).

In literature consent exists that succession poses a considerable threat to the continuity of family businesses (cp. Rosenbauer 1994, Le Mar 2001). Unsurprisingly, Reinhard Mohn of Bertelsmann described the implementation of sustainable succession solutions as the greatest entrepreneurial challenge per se (Hennerkes 1998: 374). Rosenbauer estimates that only between 10 and 15 percent of family businesses survive until third generation and less than five percent go beyond third generation (Rosenbauer 1994: 21). Specifically, the IfM Bonn estimates that almost 10 percent of all bankruptcy petitions in the SME segment are directly attributable to inadequately prepared succession (IfM Bonn 2007b).

Interestingly, most literature dedicated to *succession* in German *family businesses* focuses on tax- and legal scopes for design of the succession process (cp. Scherer 2005, Wiedmann 2002, Stephan 2002, Frank 2002, Wippenbeck 1984, Kussmaul 1983). The emphasis on tax- and legal-based aspects in the succession process is sometimes criticized. Hennerkes for example argues that the generally more important questions such as human, psychological and economic dimensions of succession are underestimated (Hennerkes 1998: 374).

Less attention in literature is paid to the fact that many family business owners tend to transfer leadership too late. Owners often are confused about alternatives, have the desire to continue achieving and fear losing control of hard-earned wealth and authority. It is not surprising then that only few family business owners plan succession systematically and in time (Huber/Sterr-Kölln 2006: 35). Only a third of European family businesses surveyed by EVCA undertook formal succession planning more than one year in advance and almost a quarter of businesses did not undergo any formal succession planning at all (EVCA 2005: 10 et sqq). Further, family business owners interestingly at first exclusively consider intergenerational succession solutions (Stracke 2005: 683).

Central to this study's research question is the *management buyout* (MBO) including associated transaction forms. While literature published in the United States and the United Kingdom related to this topical area is vast, also numerous German studies have been published in the last 20 to 25 years. Thereby these studies made use of different perspectives. The MBO concept then was often described from the viewpoint of the acquiring management (cp. Hoffmann/ Ramke 1990, Schmid 1994, Jakoby 2000 among others). Also the perspective of vendors was subject to research (cp. von Boxberg 1991, Huydts 1992 among others). Further, the method of the MBO as one instrument enabling privatisation in the new German federal states (cp. Hoffmann-Hampe 1994, Kokalj 1994 among others) and the principal development of MBO businesses ex post (Forst 1992, Luippold 1991, Achleitner/Fingerle 2003 among others) has been researched extensively.

However, few of these studies have considered the role institutional private equity assumes in the buyout process and no study has exclusively focused on private equity backed buyout scenarios in context of succession in family businesses. Although the study of Huydst (1992) to date constitutes the most comprehensive attempt to illustrate the MBO from a process perspective in context of succession in family businesses, it falls short of discussing the role of external private equity investors in the process.

Private equity in general has evolved to be a particularly favoured research topic in recent years. Among other factors, this can be attributed to the above average growth rates of new markets over the past two decades, exceptionally high returns of top performing private equity funds and increasing sizes of private equity sponsored transactions (Frommann 2003: V et sqq.). In the academic discussion addressing issues pertaining to private equity four different toeholds have emerged. The topical areas "institutional frame of the private equity market" and "alternative sources of equity financing" describe the private equity environment. An examination of private equity investments in context of buyout transactions falls in this category. The examination of the "private equity investment process" is another, arguably the most prominent research field. Studies on the "economic relevance of private equity" are typically associated with a fourth topical area.

However, the consolidation of the research disciplines pertaining to *private equity backed buyouts* and *family business succession* is still largely unexplored. Only very few empirical studies involved with the issue of succession in family businesses have considered the application and role of private equity investors in context of the succession process. To the author's knowledge only one empirical study concerned with German family businesses has made an explicit connection between institutional private equity and succession in family businesses (cp. Reimers 2004). However, this study is not exclusively concerned with succession buyouts but also investigates other investment opportunities for institutional private equity investors disassociated with succession. Further, the study has predominantly searched for process-related factors critical to the success of the private equity investment process, falling short of sufficiently weighing the impact of behavioral and psychological factors critical to success of private equity backed succession buyouts. As the author of this study proposes himself, especially these dimensions play a decisive role in the understanding of the process in the real world.

In addition, two studies have focused on longer-term effects private equity backed succession buyouts have on the targeted businesses. One of these studies was published in 2005 by EVCA in collaboration with the Center of Management Buyout Research (CMBOR) at the University of Nottingham investigating the contribution of private equity in succession of European family businesses (EVCA 2005). Here, 1,645 former family businesses in 16 European Union member countries subject to a private equity led buyout between 1994 and 2004 were surveyed. However, due to a response rate of only 7.1 percent external validity of findings is limited. The study's authors found that private equity is able to contribute both financially (e.g. monitoring of financial and operating performance, budget reporting) and non-financially (e.g. key source of contacts, recruitment and development of management, management of relationship between family owners and portfolio company management) to the succession process. In addition, the study found that targeted businesses outperformed the benchmark ex post.[3]

Similar positive effects were identified by Italian researchers (Buttignon et al. 2004). They analyzed in detail 21 large Italian family businesses of the 44 that had addressed succession through a private equity led buyout over the period 1995-2000. In their sample of family businesses employment increased on average by 31 percent between two years before and two years after the buyout. Over the same period, turnover increased by 16 percent respectively 15 percent when adjusted for inflation and industry trends. However, the results also show that the relative amount of debt in businesses subject to a private equity led succession buyout increased significantly after the buyout transaction, pointing to one of the perils generally associated with private equity led buyouts. A comparable study for Germany does not exist to date and it is questionable to what extent results for Italian businesses are transferable to German businesses.

The literature review reveals that only few studies directly related to the author's investigation have been published. The author acknowledges that the identified literature has dealt with individual aspects pertaining to private equity backed succession buyouts. In particular the studies published by EVCA (2005) and Buttignon et al. (2004) provide useful insights that allowed the author to consider and test a greater number of factors pertaining to this study's research question. However, it can be constituted that a comprehensive and validating study of private equity backed succession buyouts specific to German family businesses to date does not exist.

1.4 Research Structure

In consideration of the research context, the research objective and the state of research in the field this study will follow the research structure illustrated in figure 1.

The study is divided into six main chapters. Subsequent to this introductory chapter, *chapter 2* builds the background of this research and illuminates the topical areas family businesses, succession, private equity and success factors all

---

3 I.e. the post buyout compounded annual growth rate of turnover was 13.3 percent for reference data and 15.4 percent for survey data; the post buyout compounded annual growth rate of profit before interest and taxation (PBIT) was between 10.3 percent for reference data and 11.3 percent for survey data.

of which lie at the heart of the study's research question. Next, *chapter 3* discusses Kern's interaction theory and transaction cost theory; upon both theories the empirical data ascertainment and analysis is build. Subsequently, *chapter 4* introduces the specifications of the research method and design. *Chapter 5* makes the focal point of this study and offers a detailed analysis and discussion of the study's empirical research findings. Finally, *chapter 6* concludes in presenting a summary of results, a topical outlook and areas for future research.

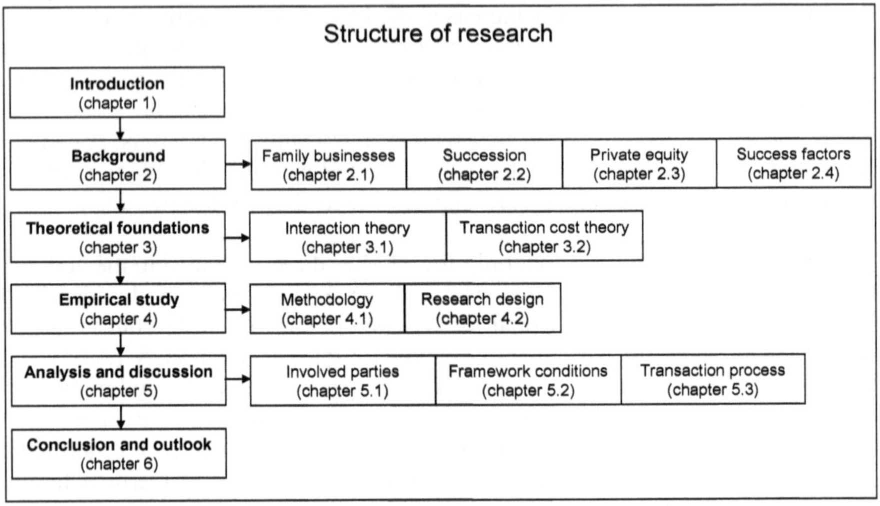

Figure 1: Research structure.
Source: Author's illustration.

2 Background

Considering the complexity of the research topic, a detailed overview and confinement of objects, terms and issues pertaining to the study's research question is indispensable. Chapter 2.1 provides an overview of family businesses in Germany. Chapter 2.2 focuses on succession and issues affecting family businesses faced with succession. Chapter 2.3 provides an introduction to private equity including the market for institutional private equity, in particular buyout capital. Finally, chapter 2.4 discusses issues pertaining to the use of the term "success" and "critical success factors" in this study.

2.1 Family businesses

For the identification of success factors in private equity backed succession buyouts in medium-sized German family businesses it is necessary to construct a working definition of the term "family businesses". Chapter 2.1.1 derives such a definition and further delineates medium-sized family businesses from family businesses of other sizes. Chapter 2.1.2 outlines the economic relevance of German family businesses while chapter 2.1.3 follows with a discussion of the financing situation of this type of businesses.

2.1.1 Definition and confinement

In order to borderline family businesses from non-family businesses both qualitative and quantitative characteristics must be used (Pfohl 1997: 4, Bontrup 1999: 105, Krimphove et al. 2003: 4). This approach accommodates the circumstance that for family businesses - due to their unique situation - unique challenges exist.

Confining characteristics of family businesses

Qualitative	Semi quantitative	Quantitative
- Legal - Ownership / liability - Leadership - Source of income a. o.	- Market structure	- Employees - Balance sheet total - Turnover - Production o. a.

Figure 2: Confining characteristics of family businesses.
Source: Author's illustration following Pfohl 1997: 4

For empirical research making use of standardized (statistical) methods the utilization of quantitative criteria obviously is indispensable due to the difficult operationalizability of qualitative attributes. Quantitative confinements typically draw on criteria such as number of employees, turnover and total assets (Krimphove et al. 2003: 4). These quantitative criteria stand out due to their favourable survey potential. For this reason the majority of empirical studies on family businesses make use of such criteria (Pfohl 1997: 14).

Table 1 displays a selection of three exemplary quantitative definitions for German small and medium-sized enterprises (SME). As the subsequent chapter (2.1.2) will show, the vast majority of these exhibit characteristics typical of family businesses. The author chose the quantitative definitions of the IfM Bonn, the European Commission and the legal definition of the German commercial code HGB (Handelsgesetzbuch).

Classification of business sizes

Size	**Employees**	**Turnover** (EUR)	**Balance sheet total** (EUR)
HGB (a minium of two criteria must be fulfilled)			
Small	< 50	< 8.030 m	< 4.015 m
Medium	< 250	< 32.120 m	< 16.060 m
Large	> 250	> 32.120 m	> 16.060 m
Institut für Mittelstandsforschung Bonn			
Small	< 10	< 1 m	-
Medium	< 500	< 50 m	-
Large	> 500	> 50 m	-
European Commission			
Smallest	< 10	either < 2 m	or < 2 m
Small	< 50	either < 10 m	or < 10 m
Medium	< 250	either < 50 m	or < 43 m

Table 1: Selection of quantitative definitions of German SME.
Source: HGB § 267, IfM Bonn 2007c, European Commission 2003: 14.

Considering the non-uniform definitions of SME, a principal delineation towards large business organizations exhibiting corporate structures appears purposeful. One option to highlight characteristics of SME is the contrasting of characteristics typical of SME with characteristics typical of corporate-type organizations. This contrasting in particular reveals what SME are not. This approach resembles a *negative delineation* (Daschmann 1994: 53). The essential structural characteristics of SME and large corporate-type organizations are contrasted in table 2.

Distinctive characteristics of SME and large (corporate) businesses

Criteria	SME	Large (corporate) businesses
Management	- Owner/Entrepreneur - Deficient flow of information - Little planning - Proximity to operations - Leadership not interchangeable	- Manager - Formalized flow of information - Extensive planning - Distance to operations - Leadership interchangeable
Organization	- Low division of labor - Short information paths - High flexibility	- High division of labour - Long (formal) information paths - Little flexibility
Turnover and employees	- Minor turnover - Few employees	- High turnover - Many employees
Purchasing and market power	Low	High
Research and development	Application-oriented, intuitive	- Application-oriented - Fundamental - Long-term - Systematic
Diversification	Low	High
Ownership Structure	Family ownership	Often dispersed ownership
Financing	- Limited access to capital market - Limited financing options	- Generally free access to capital market - Varied financing options
Governmental support	- Partial support ("Mittelstandsförderung") - Little individual support in cases of crises	- "To big to fail" syndrome, typically substantial support in cases of crisis

Table 2: Distinctive characteristics of SME and large businesses.
Source: Pfohl 1997: 19 et sqq. and Bernet et al. 2000: 23.

An analysis of legal form of German SME unveils that the legal structure is highly fragmented and that it is difficult to find variables (e.g. annual turnover, number of employees) that have predictive power with regard to legal form. However, Günterberg/Wolter (2002: 23 et sqq.) estimate that the number of partnerships (Personengesellschaften) and incorporated enterprises (Kapitalgesellschaften) among German SME with annual turnover of more than EUR 5 million is approximately equal.

While the vast majority of SME in Germany are recognized to be family businesses, the terms "SME" and "family businesses" are not synonymous. As was highlighted in table 1, SME can be confined quantitatively. In distinction, "family businesses" are predominantly characterized by the "unity of owner and business" (Hennerkes 1999: 12).

The IfM Bonn's definition of family businesses explicitly includes "unity of ownership and controllership" (IfM Bonn 2007a: 5). Here owners - constituted by ownership of the majority of voting rights - assume sole management responsibility respectively joint management responsibility with external managers. Excluded from this definition of family businesses, then, are businesses that are exclusively controlled by external managers. Also not included are businesses in which the business's top director, respectively his or her family, does not hold the majority of voting rights in the business. According to the IfM Bonn's definition, family businesses are always businesses *controlled* by its owner(s).

The unity of ownership and controllership implies that family businesses are principally independent. Family businesses are highly flexible in their decision making since no negotiation- and decision-making processes between "owners" and "controllers" (i.e. directors) are necessary.[4] The prerequisite of the unity of ownership and controllership does not imply that necessarily all decisions are initiated and executed by the business owner. Essential to the IfM Bonn's definition is that the owner maintains authority of decisions with strategic importance.[5] This is warranted if the owner or a limited number of family members also involved in management maintain control over the business, e.g. by ownership of the majority of voting rights (IfM Bonn 2007a: 6).

The operationalization of the term *family business* in this study is constituted on the basis of the IfM Bonn's definition of the term. The author acknowledges that this definition is comparatively stringent. The term family business therefore here is used in a narrow sense of possible denotations of the term.

2.1.2 Economic relevance

German SME (the German "Mittelstand") have substantially contributed to shaping the economic development in Germany after 1945. These businesses in particular were a propulsive force behind the dynamic economic development in the 1950s and 1960s (the German "Wirtschaftswunder") (Pfohl 1997: 19 et sqq).

Today approximately 3.2 million value-added tax (VAT) obligatory SME in Germany exist. According to the quantitative confinement of the IfM Bonn, only

---

4 Flexibility in the sense of the absence of reconcilement processes between principal and agent (cp. Jensen/Meckling 1976).

5 Among the decisions of strategic importance are those about the positioning in the market and against competition, add-on investments and the appointment of management personnel.

0.3 percent of these businesses earn in excess of EUR 50 million annual turnover. If the "turnover" criterion is used, this implies that 99.7 percent of all German businesses belong to the SME segment. If the "number of employees" criterion is considered, even 99.9 percent of German businesses must be included in the SME segment since these businesses employ less than 500 workers (IfM Bonn 2007a: 12 et sq.).

The aggregate number of employment relationships subject to social insurance contribution in Germany amounts to approximately 23.3 million. According to the "number of employees" criterion almost 15.4 million or 66 percent of all employment relationships are attributable to SME. If the "turnover" criterion is used, this number increases to 16.6 million respectively 70 percent. In a combined consideration of both delineation criteria - less than 500 employees and less than EUR 50 million turnover - still 14.2 million respectively 61 percent of employment relationships must be assigned to SME (IfM Bonn 2007a: 13 et sq.).

With regard to contribution to aggregate turnover of German businesses, SME add EUR 1.7 trillion (43 percent). If SME are delineated according to number of employees, this value increases substantially to 2.5 trillion (62 percent) (IfM Bonn 2007a: 15). The difference in the result of a combined use of both criteria only differs marginally from that of the sole use of the turnover criterion and therefore can be neglected.

Further Linnemann finds that SME provide approximately 80 percent of all apprenticeship training positions, contribute approximately 70 percent of all corporate taxes and pay approximately 62 percent of all welfare contributions. These findings are noteworthy considering that SME only generate less than half of German gross value added (Linnemann 2007: 7 et sqq.).

German SME are predominantly active in the business services (850,000 businesses) and trade sector (705,000 businesses) followed by businesses in construction (320,000), other public and private services (308,000), manufacturing (275,000), gastronomy (245,000) as well as communication and information transmission (127,000). In addition, 900,000 self-employed free-lance professionals need to be included (Linnemann 2007: 7). In consideration of these statistics it should be noted that the German SME segment is dominated by small businesses. Approximately 60 percent of SME in Germany have less than 10 employees (Dresdner Bank/Impulse 2002: 14). Figure 3 illustrates this circumstance in view of turnover classes.

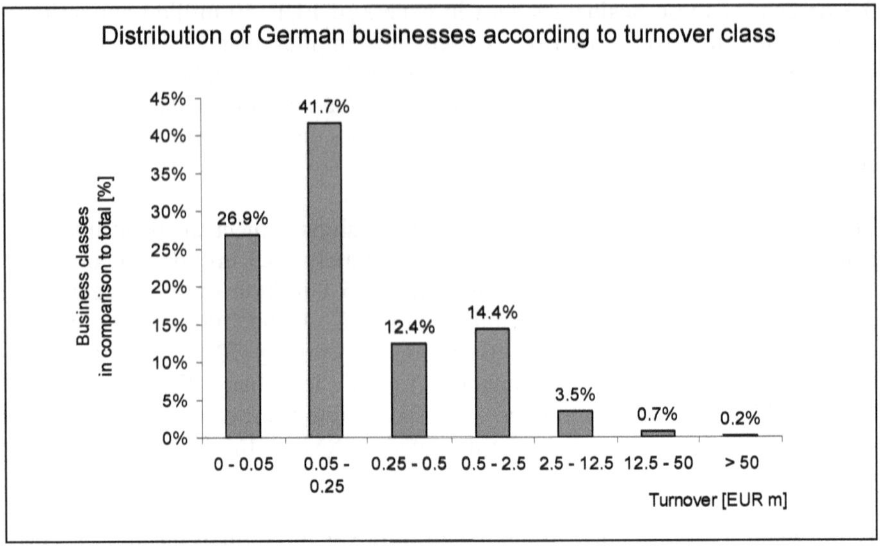

Figure 3: Distribution of German businesses according to turnover class.
Source: Schröer/Freund 1999: 5.

Conclusions about the economic relevance of *family businesses* per se - according to the narrow definition of the IfM Bonn - are difficult to make due to the difficulties associated with an adequate operationalization of the term for data collection purposes (cp. chapter 2.1.1). However, the IfM Bonn reports that approximately 3.0 million (95 percent) German businesses exhibit the unity of ownership and controllership characteristic of family businesses. The contribution to aggregate turnover of all German businesses amounts to approximately EUR 1.9 trillion (42 percent) while the provision of employment relationships subject to social insurance contribution amounts to approximately 13.4 million (57 percent) (IfM Bonn 2007a: 24). Again, the vast majority of these businesses fall into the SME segment according to the quantitative definitions outlined in the preceding chapter. Large family businesses with turnover in excess of EUR 50 million not includable in the SME segment account for only approximately 0.1 percent of all family businesses in Germany (Linnemann 2007: 4).

As these numbers indicate, the relevance of family businesses for the welfare of the German economy in particular from the perspective of employment policy is considerable. It can be concluded that family businesses not only are the dominating business type in the German business landscape but also build the primary pillar of growth and employment. Thus the solution to succession issues these businesses are facing is of critical importance not only to the affected business entities but also to the German economy at large.

2.1.3 Financing structure of German family businesses

Due to limited published information of family businesses the study of the financing structure of these businesses is difficult. In principal this is due to the dominant legal form of business partnership ("Personengesellschaft") with no or benign disclosure obligations. In addition, studies on the financing structure of German SME are based on different definitions for this type of businesses necessarily leading to varied conclusions.

The capital structure exposes the composition of the financing of a business's assets. Here, the proportion of long-term capital - in particular shareholders' equity and long-term debt - to total assets is indicative of the sustainability of the financing structure (cp. Hommel/Schneider 2003: 84).

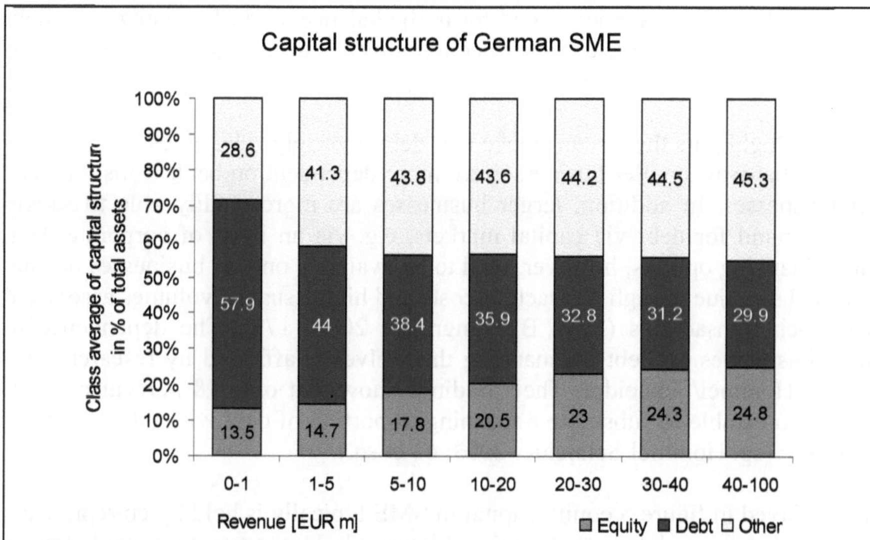

Figure 4: Capital structure of German SME.
Source: Author's illustration based on Hommel/Schneider 2003: 84.

The KfW Bankengruppe found the average equity quotas in German SME between 1996 and 2004 to be between 7 and 33 percent. Differences in the assessment are due to calculation methods (median vs. average) and different sample composition of data sources (KfW Bankengruppe 2006: 157). Nevertheless, two characteristics appear noticeable when analysing the data on equity quotas of German SME. On one hand the equity quotas are dependent on business size. Small businesses tend to have lower equity quotas while larger businesses tend to have higher equity quotas (cp. figure 4). On the other hand, equity quotas of German businesses are considerably low in international comparison. A direct comparison with equity quotas of SME in the United States and Canada shows that in Germany the equity quotas are up to 2.7 times smaller (Schefczyk 2003: 100 sqq.).

The financing structure of SME appears to be more country specific rather than contingent on industry sector, size or age. Among the primary reasons for comparatively low equity quotas in Germany arguably are the so called "house bank principle", the German bankruptcy law as well as the German tax- and accounting systems. Nevertheless, 81 percent of SME surveyed by Dresdner Bank/Impulse perceive their equity quotas to be sufficient (Dresdner Bank/ Impulse 2000: 31). A comparatively low equity endowment of German SME is also attributable to their legal form. Typically not all assets available to the business as liable capital are accounted for in the balance sheet. In comparison, debt is fully accounted for due to its tax deductibility (Deutscher Sparkassen- und Giroverband 2004a: 14).

Figure 4 highlights the circumstance that debt inversely substitutes a lack of equity. In that way smaller businesses are more dependent on bank loans than larger businesses. In addition, larger businesses are more readily able to satisfy their demand for debt via capital markets, e.g. via an issue of corporate debt. Such financing options, however, tend to be available only to businesses beyond a critical size due to high transaction costs and high issuance volumes associated with such transactions (KfW Bankengruppe 2006: 173). The dependence of small businesses on debt in financing themselves is affirmed by research findings of Hommel/Schneider. Their findings show that only 18 percent of SME believe to be able to substitute a meaningful portion of debt with other forms of financing (cp. Hommel/Schneider 2003: 63 et sq.).

As displayed in figure 5 equity capital in SME typically is held by entrepreneurs in form of majority interests. Additional interest holders are exceptionally rare in German SME. Any additional equity owners tend to hold minority interests only.

In summary, the financing situation of German SME is characterized by low equity quotas, a strong orientation towards and dependency on cashflow, a domination of (bank) debt and a low relevance of alternative forms of financing (cp. Hommel/Schneider 2003: 57). Further, SME face considerable disadvantages in financing themselves compared to large (corporate) businesses. In particular, SME have restricted access to capital markets and are constrained to accept higher capital costs (cp. European Commission 2003: 7).

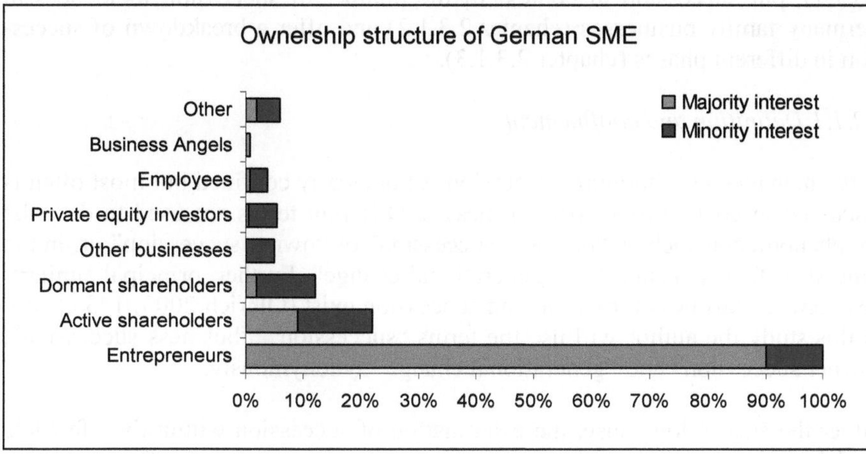

Figure 5: Shareholding structure in German SME.[6]
Source: Dresdner Bank/Impulse 2000: 23.

With regard to factors implicating the financing of German SME in the future it should be noted that banks are increasingly withdrawing from financing SME due to risk/reward considerations and increased administrative burdens (Basel II). For that reason SME are necessarily required to reassess their financing strategy. Along these developments the general acceptance among German SME to partner with institutional private equity investors is likely to grow.

2.2 Succession in family businesses

The succession process in family businesses is central to this study's investigation. For this reason this chapter features an overview of succession (chapter 2.2.1), aims to objectify and systematize the phenomenon (chapter 2.2.2) and finally outlines some of the issues typically associated with succession (chapter 2.2.3).

6 Due to the design of the study no businesses with revenue < EUR 125,000 are accounted for.

2.2.1 Overview of succession

The following chapters provide a working definition of succession (chapter 2.3.1.1), put succession in context of the number of succession incidences in Germany family businesses (chapter 2.3.1.2) and offer a breakdown of succession in different phases (chapter 2.3.1.3).

2.2.1.1 Definition and confinement

In the management literature succession is not clearly confined but most often is discussed in context of family businesses. Different terms are used to describe the phenomenon such as "business succession" or "owner succession" or, in the context of family businesses, "generational change". Further, principal similarities between business formation and succession exist (Olbrich 2003: 143 et sq.). In this study the author will use the terms "succession", "business succession", "owner succession" and "generational change" synonymously.

Either the succession cause, the examination of succession within the life cycle model of the business or the functions assigned to successors offer a starting point for confining succession (Stephan 2002: 12 et sqq.). The author first discusses rationales for succession and then uses the life cycle model of the business to describe "mature" business in order to assign private equity financing stages appropriate to finance succession in subsequent chapters. However, most useful appears the characterisation of succession with the help of functions assigned to the successor.

Central to the observation of succession in family businesses is the change of both ownership and controllership. Succession thus is realizable disregardless of whether the business is owned by a single individual, a group of family members or a dispersed group of interest holders. Although this study is exclusively concerned with succession in family businesses, a restriction of the phenomenon to family businesses only generally leads to negligence of other businesses also affected (Olbrich 2003: 134).

In the vast majority of SME controllership is assumed by the owner, his/her family or other proprietors (cp. chapter 2.1.1). Only a minority of approximately 3 percent of SME are directed by an externally hired manager or in conjunction with an externally hired manager (cp. Dresdner Bank/Impulse 2002: 15). Also the transfer of less than 100 percent of ownership rights can constitute succession, in particular if ownership is dispersed. However, a change in ownership rights without a concurrent change in controllership can not constitute succession in the strict denotation of the term. Such change in ownership rights would merely constitute an exchange similar to the transfer of shares on the stock market. Borderline cases, however, exist such as asset stripping as well as business liquidation (Olbrich 2003: 137 et sq.).

For this study the author considers succession to be constituted by the transfer of ownership *and* controllership to one or more new owner(s). Further it should be noted that a transfer of less than 100 percent of ownership rights might constitute succession as long as the departing owner(s) assumed controllership and if controllership is transferred to new owner(s).

Since private equity (and in particular venture capital) financings are often under examination in context of business formation (cp. chapter 2.3.2.1) a confinement of *business succession* next to *business formation* appears feasible. According to Hering/Olbrich business formation must be differentiated by the circumstances of the formation (Hering/Olbrich 2003: 9 et sq). Principally, it is possible to differentiate between a *proprietary formation* and a *formation by external procurement.* In cases of proprietary formation the business is set up by an entrepreneur, also describable as "build-up formation" or "original formation". On the other hand, if controllership is acquired by external procurement, the business formation needs to be qualified as "acquisition formation" or "derivative formation". Four typical scenarios in the context of business formation and business succession are distinguishable (Hering/Olbrich 2003: 11 et sqq.):

(1) *Succession and formation*: This is the "standard" scenario in business succession. Essential here is the choice of perspective, i.e. the perspective of the transferor or transferee.

(2) *Succession but no formation*: In this case ownership rights are transferred from one hand to a number of different economic entities. However, no single entity receives controllership (e.g. initial public offering on the stock market).

(3) *No succession but acquisition formation*: Here different economic entities transfer ownership rights to one economic entity. One example could be the delisting of a business from a stock market and the acquisition of outstanding stocks by one acquirer.

(4) *No succession and no acquisition formation*: If a minority interest in a business is transferred without transfer of significant controllership neither a succession nor an acquisition formation is warranted (e.g. equity trading on the stock market).

Figure 6 gives an overview of the possible constellations of business succession and business formation on the basis of controllership.

Classification of succession forms

New owner \ Existing owner	Controllership	No controllership
Controllership	1 Business succession, acquisition formation	3 No business succession, acquisition formation
No controllership	2 Business succession, no acquisition formation	4 No business succession, no acquisition formation

Figure 6: Confinement of business succession and business formation.
Source: Author's illustration.

It can be constituted that business succession in many incidences assumes characteristics of a business formation, as is the case for a buyout succession scenario. As will be discussed in subsequent chapters, this insight receives accentuation in context of the screening of successor candidates for suitability.

2.2.1.2 Succession in numbers

Only limited data on succession in German family businesses are available. Further, the data available have only limited representativeness and is not collected periodically. However, it can be assumed that approximately 70 percent of German family businesses aim for succession within the family (Hennerkes 1998: 375). This circumstance must limit the chances for realizing sustainable succession from the start, especially since the motivation of successor candidates from within the family to assume leadership responsibility has decreased considerably over the years (Hennerkes 1998: 375). In at least half of all succession incidences no family member is willing or able to succeed the incumbent business owner. Leastwise every second succession therefore is realized by a non-family succession route.

Presumably, the IfM Bonn is the most trustable source with regard to succession data pertaining to German family businesses. Their most recent statistic on succession incidences is based on a population of 90,431 German family businesses that fitted their research criteria.[7] The IfM Bonn calculated that in the period from 2005-2009 approximately 345,000 businesses attempt to realize succes-

---

7 Included in the study are businesses with the following characteristics: turnover < EUR 100 million, < 500 employees, owner has controllership.

sion. This corresponds to approximately 71,900 succession incidences p.a. It is expected that of these incidences 44 percent are realized within the family while another 21 percent of businesses are expected to be sold to strategic investors (e.g. competitors). 27 percent of all transferred businesses are expected to sustain existence – but also their specific culture and independence – by means of a MBO or MBI. This amounts to more than 19,000 businesses p.a. (IfM Bonn 2007b).

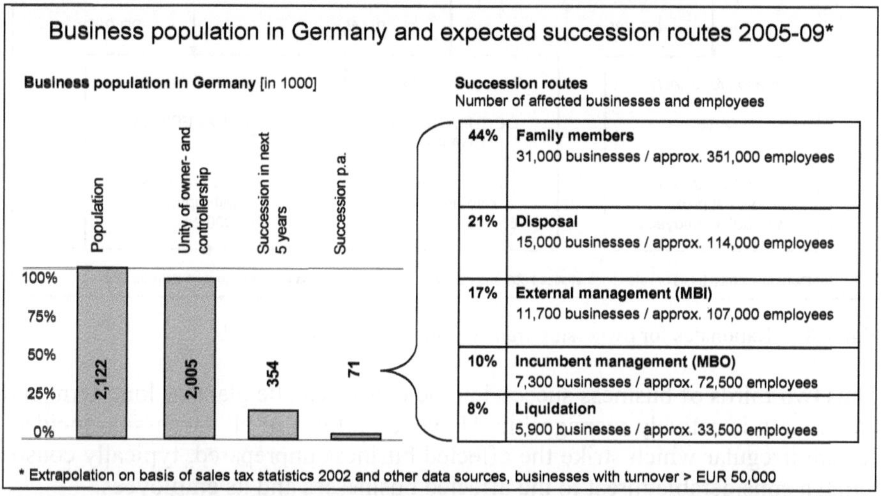

Figure 7: Succession routes in German family businesses.
Source: IfM Bonn 2007b.

Rationales for business succession break down to ordinary, planned succession, which constitutes the normal case, as well as unplanned succession (Stephan 2002: 12). According to the IfM Bonn, 66 percent of businesses are transferred due to age and thus the transfer can be planned in advance. The principal reason for irregular, unplanned succession is the unexpected withdrawal of owners (e.g. due to health issues to the point of demise) which constitute 26 percent of all succession events. A third reason that is also difficult to plan for in advance is the transfer of ownership due to new occupational endeavours of the business owner (8 percent of all events) attributable to conflict within the family, divorce or alternative plans for the future (IfM Bonn 2007b, Schröer/Freund 1999: 14). An overview of rationales for ownership transfer is illustrated in figure 8.

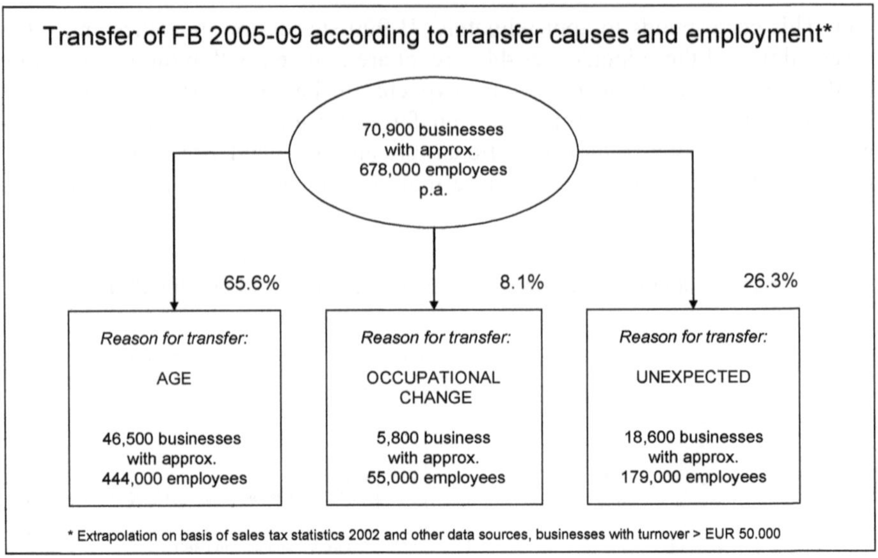

Figure 8: Rationales for ownership transfer. Source: IfM Bonn 2007b.

Thus two thirds of business succession incidences can be planned long-term and the process is actively manageable. However, a third of all succession incidences are irregular which strike the affected business unprepared, typically constituting a considerable threat to the affected businesses and its employees.

2.2.1.3 Phases of succession

Succession is a complex process that varies considerably from case to case. Succession in the broader sense demands a planning horizon of three to five years. In this period the planning and transaction of succession is realized. Nevertheless, an additional period of preparation and postprocessing is typically unavoidable (Schließmann/Fandrich 2001: 374 et sqq.; Stephan 2002: 43).

From a process perspective, succession can be divided in four constitutive phases that lead to the final handover of the business (Stephan 2002: 167 et sqq.):

(1) Appraisal: After recognition of the necessity for succession family business owners are urged to identify and establish contact with potential successors. After analysis of the starting position of the business as well as the particular situation of successors and transferors joint objectives for succession are deduced. Typically the objectives of successors and transferors differ considerably. This

explains the failure of many succession processes at an early stage when objectives of the involved are incommensurate (Felden/Klaus 2003: 59). However, common ground for both successors and transferors appears to be the long-term continuity of the business subject to succession. In this context the safeguarding of jobs, the quality of successor(s) and the perpetuation of unity in ownership and controllership typically are high-ranking among transferors (IfM Mannheim 2003: 15 et sqq.).

(2) Preparation: At this stage the transferor must select among different succession routes (cp. chapter 2.2.2.1) unless only one succession alternative is available and realizable (Stephan 2002: 11 et sq.). For most succession alternatives both transferors and successors start to attend to their respective assignments, e.g. the orientation and qualification of successor(s), the examination of financing aspects, as well as the design of an emergency plan for the untimely departure of the transferor. Depending on the size of the business and the complexity of the succession process consultants might be involved to mitigate risks associated with succession processes. Principal assignments of succession consultants circle around the facilitation of frictionless succession processes, the mediation between transferors and successors as well as the contribution of specialized expertise. Oftentimes succession consultants also facilitate the establishment of contacts to potential successors (Huber/Sterr Kölln 2006: 33 et sqq.).

(3) Conceptualization: Central attention in this phase of the succession process pertains to the acceptance of joint management responsibility of the transferor and the successor with the objective of testing and developing the successor's suitability. Through the incremental transfer of leadership responsibility insecurities and loss of orientation that necessarily are associated with the departure of the incumbent owner is reduced (Stephan 2002: 43). In addition, a period of joint work experience reduces information asymmetries between transferors and successors (Stephan 2002: 60 et sq.). However, in particular the conceptualization phase is characterized by increased potential for conflict. This is primarily due to shared but often not clearly delineated leadership responsibility. Further, typically a catalogue of duties and assignments of involved fixed to a time schedule is defined and agreed on. At last, after contractual agreements are resolved and both parties are sufficiently interested to execute the transfer, a sales contract is closed (Felden/Klaus 2003: 64).

(4) Realization: In this phase the actual succession is implemented signified by the transfer of ownership rights from transferors to successors. Transferors successively withdraw from business operations and potentially alternate to advisory board positions. Subsequently, strategic repositioning or structural changes are common. This might be accompanied e.g. by strategic repositioning, altered

human resources planning or new communication methods (Schröer/ Freund 1999: 77). Now a considerable coordination effort for succession planning - which affects all relevant planning efforts of the firm - becomes necessary (cp. figure 9). One example of such coordination effort is the assurance of liquidity in line with other financial- and investment planning of the business subject to succession. The coordination among transferors and successor in this respect is of particular importance.

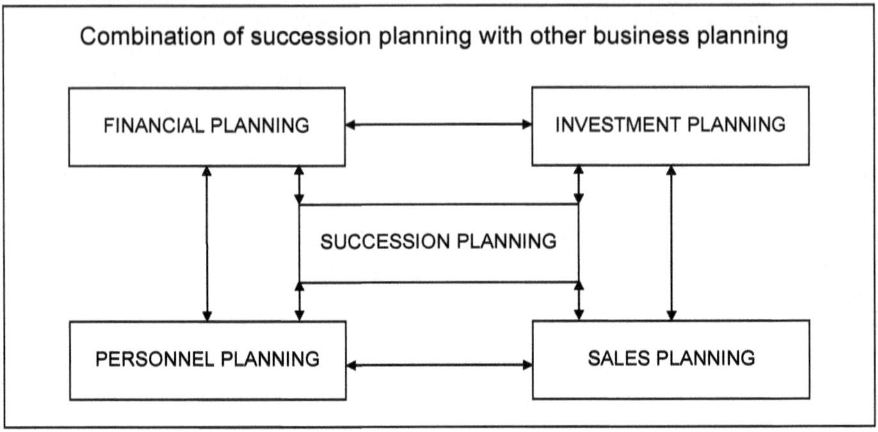

Figure 9: Succession planning and other business planning.
Source: Stephan 2002: 167 et sq.

It appears that succession is a process necessarily driven by both transferors and successors. Thereby a period of joint management responsibility is inevitable. As chapter 5 will show, the transfer of knowledge from transferor to successor is of critical importance in realizing success in private equity backed succession buyouts. In this sense, a period of joint management control - despite its inherent conflict potential - turns out to be functional.

2.2.2 Systematization of succession

Three fundamental if similar characteristics of succession need to be differentiated. First, the *transfer of assets* according to civil law; second, the *form of succession* that results from the asset transfer and constitution of successors; third, the *payment method* which characterizes the reciprocation of successors in return for transferred assets. This chapter specifically focuses on succession forms (2.2.2.1) and their characteristics (2.2.2.2).

2.2.2.1 Succession forms

For the characterization of different succession forms these are first differentiated and systematized. Subsequently, conclusions about successors and conclusions with regard to financing requirements associated with different succession forms are possible.

Succession forms are readily differentiated according to civil law characteristics. This is inheritance, beneficence, trust or sale in accordance with the transfer of assets described in the German HGB (Hering/Olbrich 2003: 63 et sqq.). The actual succession forms also refer to the origin of the successor as well as the provision of asset transfer. These differences are illustrated in table 3.

Forms of succession and characteristics in overview

Asset transfer / Characteristics	Inheritance	Beneficence	Trust	Sale
Reciprocation of beneficiary	Gratuitous, inheritance tax due	Gratuitous, accessions tax due	Gratuitous, in case of family trust inheritance tax and accessions tax due	Gratuitous, purchase price as lump sum or recurring benefit
Type of transferring proprietor	Natural person	Natural person or institutional proprietor	Natural person or institutional proprietor	Natural person or institutional proprietor
Point in time for natural person as proprietor	In case of death	In life	In life or case of death	In life
Forms of succession	Intra-family succession: - Family members assume management - External management		- Family trust - Charitable trust - Hybrid forms	- MBO - MBI - IPO

Table 3: Forms of succession and characteristics in overview.
Source: Hering/Olbrich 2003: 63 et sqq.

Based on this categorization three principal succession routes with practical relevance can be differentiated. This is (1) intra-family succession, (2) sale to internal- or external managers as well as (3) sale to third parties. The author passes on a further discussion of the establishment of trusts since they only concern a negligible portion of succession incidences in Germany (Schröer/ Freund 1999: 8).

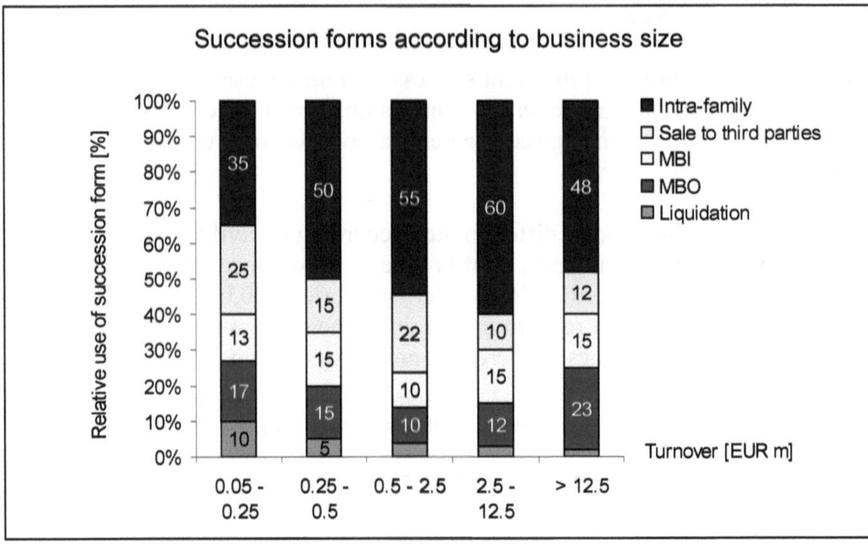

Figure 10: Succession forms according to business size.
Source: Schröer/Freund 1999: 22

Figure 10 illustrates the distribution of succession forms in Germany according to business size. Also in this illustration a prevalence of intra-family succession is obvious. However, as was already indicated, forms of succession outside the family are becoming increasingly relevant. According to a recent IfM Bonn survey the main reason for opting for non-family succession is not attributable to the non-existence of family successors but the lack of interest of potential family successors to assume leadership responsibility (almost 61 percent of respondents) or that family business owners do not have sufficient confidence in the qualifications of their offspring (17 percent of respondents) (IfM Bonn 2005). However, the willingness of potential successors from within the family to assume leadership responsibility appears to increase proportionally with the business's size. This phenomenon can be explained with the stronger earning power and superior attractiveness of assignments within larger businesses.

Sharma and Irving have noticed that successors from within the family join their family business for different reasons and have identified four different mind-sets that drive their commitment to succeed the parent: *(1) affective* (based on desire), *(2) normative* (based on obligation), *(3) calculative* (based on opportunity costs) and *(4) imperative* (based on need) (Sharma/Irving 2005: 13). However, while intergenerational succession within the family is the premier choice among the majority of family business owners, clearly not always family members are sufficiently qualified or competent to make a positive contribution to their family business (cp. 2.2.3.1).

For that reason succession forms that constitute business divesture or liquidation amount to up to half of all succession incidences in Germany (Schröer/Freund 1999: 20 et sqq.).

2.2.2.2 Characteristics of succession forms

(1) Intra-family schemes of succession: Intra family succession is constituted if either family members or external parties assume controllership of the business subject to succession. Critical precondition, however, is that ownership continues to be in family hand. In order to implement one or more external manager a minimum size of the business appears necessary due to remuneration considerations. A business that is family-owned but managed by external managers necessarily implies a softening of the unity of ownership and controllership. Nevertheless, owners might be able to exercise influence through advisory or supervisory boards (Schließmann/Fandrich 2001: 118 et sqq.). It is also conceivable that an external manager or management team is recruited for a limited period of time in order to bridge time for the training and qualification of family candidates. Succession within the family presupposes the availability of a qualified family successor. As illustrated in figure 10, approximately half of all family business successions are intra-family successions.

The asset transfer here typically occurs by inheritance should the transferor has perished or by beneficence in lifetime. Typically both of these succession varieties are gratuitous, e.g. the beneficiary has no obligation to compensate the transferor financially. Nevertheless, tax implications need to be considered (Hering/Olbrich 2003: 63) as well as potential claims of other family members and heirs settled.

(2) Buyout schemes of succession: Different succession forms involving the sale to incumbent or external managers exist. If the incumbent management acquires all or parts of a business subject to succession the transaction is characteristic of a management buyout (MBO). In case of the classic MBO an instantaneous acquisition of all outstanding ownership rights is transacted. In a strict sense, the transfer of a minority interest to the incumbent management does not constitute a MBO. However, a buyout in "instalments" is certainly practicable. Consequently the MBO can appear in number of different forms. Notable advantages of MBOs are that the incumbent management is typically intimately familiar with the business and less information asymmetries between transferors and successors exist compared to other non-family succession schemes. Unfavour-

able in this context, however, is the circumstance that the management in family businesses with a paternalistic owner often is not sufficiently patronized and for that reason oftentimes lacks qualification (Schließmann/Fandrich: 2001: 123). Approximately 10 to 20 percent of all successions in German SME are MBOs as illustrated in figure 10.

In difference to the MBO, the management buyin (MBI) is characterized by acquisition of ownership rights by an external management. Notable advantage of this succession form is the impartiality of external managers and their ability to complement know-how potentially lacking within the business subject to succession. Disadvantageous on the other hand necessarily is the lack of intimate knowledge of the business compared to an incumbent management team. Otherwise the MBO and MBI feature similar characteristics (Schließmann/ Fandrich 2001: 123). Depending on business size, approximately 10 – 25 percent of succession incidences are MBIs (cp. figure 10). A number of additional varieties such as the buyin management buyout (BIMBO), the employee buyout or the spin-off exist. However, especially the later two have little relevancy in the context of succession in family businesses. Nevertheless, a clear-cut detachment among these schemes often is not possible (Schließmann/Fandrich 2001: 124).

Conditions of the asset transfer in buyout succession schemes are agreed on in the purchase agreement and are non-gratuitous in almost 3/4 of all cases (cp. table 3). Depending on the terms of the transaction the payment obligation of the acquirer might be settled in form of a recurring or non-recurring payment. The financial burden on the acquiring management - especially in context of purchase of larger businesses - is substantial. Only in very rare cases the buyout management team is able to fund the transaction exclusively with private wealth. As a consequence, the realization of MBO/MBI transactions to a large extent depends on outside equity and/or debt investors (Weber-Rey 2001: 603, Schließmann/Fandrich 2001: 123).[8]

(3) Sale to third parties: Strategic buyers typically are competitors that have a strategic interest in acquiring the business subject to succession. In comparison to other succession schemes the confidence building between transferor and acquirer typically is more difficult, time intensive and characterized by numerous pitfalls. This predominantly must be associated with uncertainty regarding the other party's commitment to close the transaction. This uncertainty can be particular harmful to the transferor if the potential acquirer withdraws from the acquisition process but is able to obtain and exploit sensitive data and trade secrets

8 For a continuative discussion of MBOs and MBIs refer to chapter 2.3.3.

during and after the process. For this reason the closure of contractual agreements specifying penalties and confidentiality is of special importance in context of this succession scheme. Principally the acquisition can be completed in one- or successively in several steps. Typically, however, a sale to a strategic buyer is completed at once in order to limit conflict potential. Here and in some cases of buyout succession schemes the transferors commonly are asked to continue to serve the business in a consultative- or advisory board function (Schließmann/Fandrich 2001: 125 et sqq.). Contingent on business size, every fourth to tenth succession incidence in German SME constitutes a sale to a strategic buyer (cp. figure 10).

Three principal motives are conceivable why a strategic buyer might be interested to acquire a business facing succession. If the investment return is the target criterion the acquirer acts out of pure financial considerations. Next, the acquisition could occur out of capacity considerations with the objective of merging or integrating the acquired businesses. In this case the value of the business corresponds to the investment return and the synergetic advantages of the merger. The third acquisition motive is of strategic nature with the long-term objective of establishing a particular market position. The value of the business to the acquirer then is contingent on future earnings and strategic use (European Commission 2002: 50 et sq.).

The asset transfer here and in the aforementioned buyout schemes occurs by means of acquisition. The purchase price might be paid in one or several increment(s). However, due to the aforementioned problems associated with trust building among transaction partners, transferors typically demand lump sum payments (cp. Hering/Olbrich 2003: 63, Schließmann/Fandrich 2001: 125 et sqq.).

Table 4 summarizes advantages and disadvantages typically associated with the succession schemes introduced above.

Advantages / disadvantages associated with non-family succession schemes		
	Advantages	***Disadvantages***
Strategic investor	• Generation of additional business • Realization of synergies • Understanding for industry and business know-how • Purchase price	• Financing possibly difficult • Exertion of influence desired • Typically majority shareholding • Discretion not warranted
Financial investor	• Exercise of influence on daily operations limited • High financial power • Distinct experience in structuring transactions • Discretion	• Limited impulses for operative business • Exit preset • High cash-out • Interested in relatively quick and high return
MBO / MBI	• Corporate structure typically is maintained • Understanding for industry and business know-how • Discretion	• Limited financial resources • Typically in combination with private equity investor • Negotiation of purchase price

Table 4: Advantages and disadvantages of succession schemes.
Source: Author's illustration.

2.2.3 Issues

Succession failure has considerable consequences for the family business's internal and external stakeholders. As figure 11 shows, succession failure effects not only the business's direct owner(s) and employees but also financial intermediaries providing debt financing, suppliers, customers, competitors and the larger social system the business is embedded in.

Considering the far-reaching implications of succession failure and -success it appears necessary to discuss the most relevant problem areas in context of succession. Next to general succession related issues facing most family businesses at some point in time, the focus here in particular lies on economic and financial problems exacerbating the succession process. The discussion aims to show that the issue of financing assumes a pivotal role in realizing succession. Despite the number and weight of problems discussed in the following section it should be noted that succession may also offer prospects for promising change in affected businesses.

Implications of succession failure and success in family businesses

	Stakeholder	Implications of failed succession	Implications of successful succession
Internal stakeholders	- Owner	- Liquidation of business, loss of professional existence	- Securing and/or augmenting the business's value and the value of the business's shares, ability to distribute company profits, self-affirmation
	- Shareholders within family	- Loss of family wealth, threat of inadequate supply for family	
	- Shareholders outside family	- Value depreciation of equity holdings, loss of social standing, psychological damage	
	- Employees	- Loss of job, possibly value depreciation of equity holdings, loss of social standing, psychological damage	- Security of employment, potentially value appreciation of equity holdings
External stakeholders	- Debt providers	- Full or partial default on loans, delayed loan redemption	- Intensifying and/or extension of business volume
	- Suppliers	- Full or partial loss of commercial consumer	- Commercial consumption of service(s)/product(s) prevails
	- Customers	- Full or partial loss of delivery	- Delivery of service(s)/product(s) prevails
	- Competitors/branch	- Threat to credit status of industry branch	- Enhancement of image of industry branch
	- State/government	- Tax deficit	- Additional tax receipts

Figure 11: Implications of succession failure and success.
Source: Author's illustration.

2.2.3.1 General issues

The preceding chapter highlighted which succession alternatives generally are available to family business owners. However, in context of succession manifold problems may arise.

With regard to intra-family succession it is observable that family business owner's offspring often are simply not of sufficient age at the time of the owner's retirement to assume leadership responsibility (Albach/Freund 1989: 22). On the other hand, the owner's children are typically much less enthusiastic about the perpetuation of the family business than the owner him-/herself. Luippold finds that the idea of keeping up family tradition, which used to be strongly accentuated and which made entrance into the family business compelling, increasingly has lost in weight among younger generations. More important rather are oftentimes to achieve high incomes as well as a free development of personality. Next to the lack of competency, in some cases an often overbearing dominance of the departing generation will discourage potential family successors (Luippold 1991: 159). Finally, provided that family members are willing and able to succeed, these must often deal with complicated ownership ratios if other siblings and other family members have inherited ownership- and voting rights and are able to influence business decisions of strategic importance.

Considering further decreasing birth rates, the number of potential successors within the family diminishes. Also the cumulative academization increases the probability of the owner's retirement before the offspring is actually able to succeed the parent. Moreover, considering that in 90 percent of cases in which family members are both interested and in the right age to assume leadership, succession is not or only insufficiently arranged for (cp. Albach/Freund 1989: 265), it becomes obvious that the transfer of leadership within the family is likely to assume less relevance in the future. The bottom line of the comprehensive analysis by Albach/Freund even reads: "The family business dies out"" (Albach/Freund 1989: 264).

Different empirical studies indicate that succession in approximately 1/3 of affected family businesses does not shape up as initially planned, developing into a serious existential crisis. These surveys indicate that succession is among the most significant sources of crisis in family businesses (Freund 2000: 1, Rapp 1996: 7 et sq., Bechtle 1983). Problems are accentuated in cases in which the business owner withdraws unexpectedly due to illness, mischance or death (Freund et al. 1995: 37).

On the side of *transferors* two categories of factors causing failure in succession can be differentiated. On one hand these are factors caused by a lack of planning and preparing for succession in due time. Particularly problematic are the lack of promotion of new blood and oftentimes the absence of a second management layer. Often the transferor is addressing succession issues too late; sometimes so late that restructuring measures need to be implemented by successors. In some cases succession is completely left to chance (EVCA 2005: 11 et sq.). The high dependency of the family business' wellbeing on the person of the owner and thus the related "missing exchangeability of the leadership potential" (Pfohl 1997: 18) augments the problem of the non-existence of a succession plan startling common in family businesses.

The second category of factors relates to the common phenomenon of the transferors' inability to 'let go'. Here it can be observed that transferors often lack occupation and perspective post transfer of the business (Schröer/Freund 1999: 56 et sq.). Also the high level of emotional involvement of transferors in the succession process can pose manifold problems (Huber/Sterr-Kölln 2006: 15). In some cases the business's true economic situation is concealed and incomplete or false information is issued. Despite the commonness of these issues surprisingly they have not found their way to the business literature in any appreciable way. Reasons for this noteworthy circumstance might be attributable to the more psychological/sociological character of these problems and/or their difficult access.

Reasons for succession failure on the *side of successors* must be linked to a lack of aptitude. Often successors have insufficient leadership or industry sector experience. Further, external managers might have problems dealing with challenges distinct to family businesses. This holds true especially if these managers come from a large, corporate-type organization. A further common problem in particular external managers are faced with is a lack of willingness to cooperate and low acceptability of successors among incumbent employees (Schröer/Freund 1999: 57 et sq.).

Furthermore, numerous reasons for succession failure that are best described as management faults exist. Both transferors and/or successors might be responsible for management faults. These are generally flaws in the business policy of the firm, e.g. a high degree of person-centric orientation of the business if success is attributed to the transferor and not the whole business organization. In this case a considerable loss in image and trust on the side of customers and suppliers can not be ruled out (Schröer/Freund 1999: 58). Around half of all failures in succession can be related to psychological-emotional issues. The existent main problem areas here are goal-, appraisal-, role-, allocation-, and method conflicts (cp. Felden/Klaus 2003: 148).

Also, performance of the business ex post may depend on the level of frictions in the succession process itself. If both transferor and successor are not satisfied with the process, the agreed on (and in some instances contracted) behavior may not be exhibited ex post. E.g. the performance of the transferred business may be retarded if the successor is unable to incentivize the retired owner to transfer tacit knowledge (i.e. knowledge that is only known to the owner and difficult to share), provide legitimacy or maintain crucial business relationships with former loyal customers and suppliers (Howorth et al. 2004: 513).

The causes for succession failure addressed above are relevant to situations in which a successor is already identified. However, due to the incompleteness of the market for external successors often a suitable successor can not be identified in due course. Identifying suitable successor candidates outside the family and outside the family business often is associated with significant time- and monetary expenditures to the extent that some authors are describing the phenomenon as market failure for external business succession. In particular this affects small businesses with turnover of less than EUR 2.5 million (Schröer/

Freund 1999: 82). In general it is observable that the larger the businesses subject to succession, the higher the prospects of realizing promising, sustainable succession solutions (European Commission 2002: 50).

The general challenges introduced in this chapter highlight the increasing relevance of non-family succession forms such as MBOs and MBIs. The typical reasons for succession failure directly associable with either transferors or successors also apply to private equity backed succession buyouts and will be analyzed in more detail in chapter 5.

2.2.3.2 Issues related to economic and financial challenges

A large portion of issues posing problems in the succession process are related to financial challenges. These are particularly prevalent in non-family succession scenarios; approximately every second non-family succession is affected. This makes financing the business acquisition rank top of all challenges experienced by non-family successors (cp. IfM Mannheim 2003: 42).

From the perspective of successors the most common cause of financing difficulties is insufficient capital resources. This is followed by affiliation of the targeted business with a troubled industry sector, the lack of collateral, emerging unexpected capital requirements as well as other causes. The causes of financing difficulties are contrasted in figure 12.

These findings are also supported by Schröer/Freund. The essential problem among successors is their financial impotence. Accordingly they often experience difficulties in financing the demanded purchase price and succession might fail despite existent aptitude of successor candidates. However, in some cases financial issues on the side of transferors might be inhibiting succession. This might be the case if the transferor holds excessive and unrealistic price expectation (Schröer/Freund 1999: 57).

Also for intra-family succession schemes financial challenges exist, in particular in relation to compensation claims of yielding heirs and tax (i.e. accessions- and capital transfer tax) issues. These issues typically demand substantial liquidity that needs to be financed without weakening the financial position of the transferred business (Schließmann/Fandrich 2001: 4 et sq.).

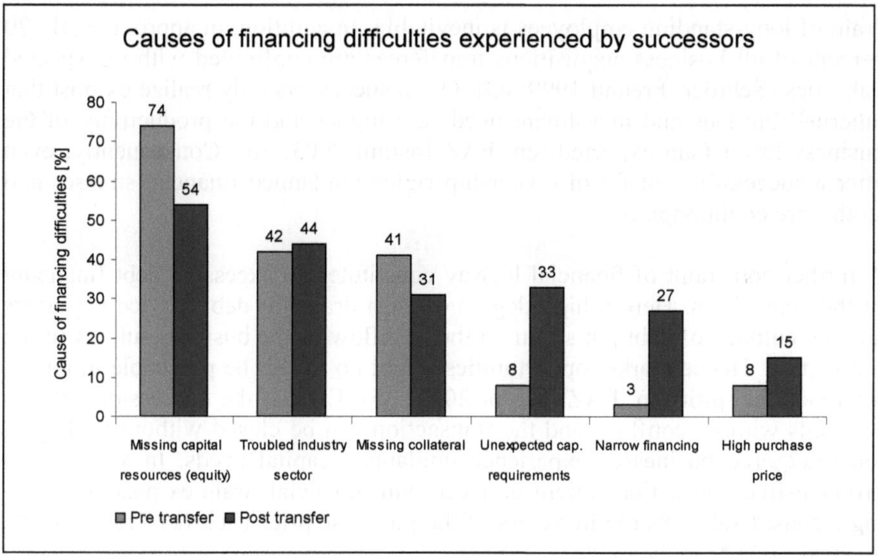

Figure 12: Causes of financing difficulties for successors.
Source: IfM Mannheim 2003: 43.

Due to the limited amount of equity available to typical successor candidates, a considerable portion of the purchase price is necessarily obtained by conventional *debt financing*. The appraisal of the credit potential is determined by the unutilized collateral[9] as well as excess liquidity surplus usable for debt service purposes. In context of the maximal possible borrowing capacity it is important to note that in the course of generational change - due to the loss of personal goodwill of the departing owner - a re-evaluation of the bank's debt engagement is common. The specified credit potential thus foremost is comparable to the expected, free liquidity surplus in order to determine to what extent debt service payments along the aimed for amortization plan are possible (Bergamin 1995:55).

Post-transfer problems may arise that must be assigned to the succession process itself. In approximately ¾ of all successions indications emerge ex post that the economic situation of the transferred business is less advantageous than assumed ex ante. In almost half of all businesses undergoing succession a break-up or

9 The additional possible debt potential is determined by the sum of maximal commonly accepted collateral exploitation per asset position, less already existent debt and long-term liabilities.

drain of long-standing employees is inevitable. In addition, in approximately 20 percent of all business acquisitions transferees are confronted with unexpected liabilities (Schröer/ Freund 1999: 63). Often successors only realize ex post that inherited burdens and investment needs are higher and the productivity of the business lower than expected (cp. FAZ Institut 2003: 36). Consequently, even after a successful transfer of ownership rights unplanned financial stresses and strains are commonplace.

A further constraint of financial leeway constitutes an excessive debt financing of the acquisition. Here a high degree of cash drain for debt service payments and the cutback of debt put strain on the cashflow of the business subject to the transaction. Hence market opportunities might no longer be pursuable in an entrepreneurial spirit (cp. FAZ Institut 2003: 35). Even if the succession process proceeds without conflicts and the transaction can be closed without problems, most acquired businesses experience unplanned capital needs. In so far, also problem-free transactions might be faced with financial strain ex post constituting a considerable charge in excess of the purchase price (Schröer/Freund 1999: 80 et sq.; IfM Mannheim 2003: 42).

In summary, it can be stated that the financing of succession is among the central challenges facing successors. Due to low equity quotas and the exhaustion of debt financing potential typical to many German family businesses, non-family successors are constrained to insert significant amounts of equity into the succession transaction. The procurement of external sources of equity capital thus often is at the fore of successfully realizing succession. This implies that both transferors and successors must address this challenge and close possible financing gaps.

2.3 Private Equity

While the previous chapter ascribed one central challenge associated with succession in family businesses to the lack of financial potency of (non-family) successor candidates, this chapter introduces private equity which has the potential to contribute to the resolution of the issue. First, characteristics particular to private equity financings are introduced (chapter 2.3.1), followed by a more detailed overview of private equity backed buyouts (chapter 2.3.2) and the German market for private equity backed buyouts (chapter 2.3.3).

2.3.1 Classification and confinement

Private equity is typically associated with equity capital provided to enterprises not listed on a stock market. Private equity can be used to develop new products and technologies, expand working capital, make acquisitions, or strengthen a business's balance sheet. It may also resolve ownership and management issues. Succession in family businesses or the buyout and buyin of a business by experienced managers may be achieved using private equity funding. According to the conception of most authors, venture capital is, strictly speaking, a subset of private equity and refers to equity investments made for the launch, early development, or expansion of a business. Figure 13 exhibits a simplified overview of varieties of private equity.

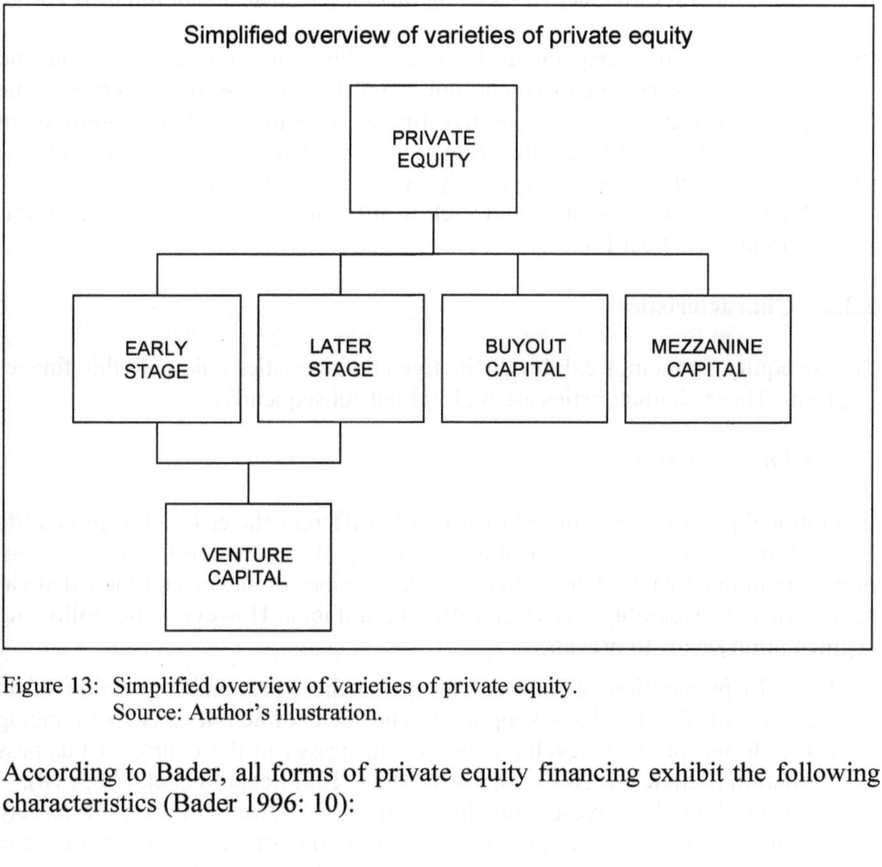

Figure 13: Simplified overview of varieties of private equity.
Source: Author's illustration.

According to Bader, all forms of private equity financing exhibit the following characteristics (Bader 1996: 10):

(1) Private equity is a method of financing, not a finance instrument.
(2) Private equity investments are investments in (private) businesses not listed on a stock market.
(3) Private equity investments most often provide equity capital to the receiving businesses. However, structures involving debt- or mezzanine capital - a hybrid of equity and debt - are possible to achieve more flexibility (e.g. tax advantages, no change of ownership structure etc.).
(4) Private equity investments are future-oriented. Businesses receiving private equity funding are in a critical phase of their development. Return expectations of the private equity investor justify the risk associated with the investment.
(5) Private equity capital is relatively costly and is typically provided when the collateral of the capital-seeking business is insufficient to borrow from a bank.
(6) Private equity engagements have a medium- to long-term horizon and typically last between two and ten years. In any case the objective of the private equity investor is the divesture of its equity holding at some point in time. Often the divesture strategy is defined prior to an engagement.
(7) Private equity investors typically accompany and provide advice to the businesses they invest in and seek to influence decisions of strategic importance via board seats.

2.3.2 Characteristics

Private equity financings exhibit distinctive characteristics unique to this financing form. These characteristics are highlighted subsequently.

2.3.2.1 Financing stages

Institutional private equity investors invest in different stages of a business's life cycle. A precise confinement of these financing stages (also referred to as segments) is impracticable. Unsurprisingly, the number of stages and their denotation varies considerably between different authors. However, the following segmentation seems to prevail:

- *Seed:* In preparation of business inception the aging and realization of an idea in utilizable results is supported. The focus of activities is on financing research and product development for businesses in the course of business formation (Schefczyk 2006: 24, Bader 1996: 105, Leopold et al. 2003: 18).
- *Start-up:* Includes investments in business formation. In case of largely completed product development the focus is on first marketing efforts and preparation of production facilities; financed businesses have typically not

marketed products yet (Schefczyk 2006: 24, Bader 1996: 105, Leopold et al. 2003: 18).

- *Expansion:* Includes financing the start of production or business expansion for businesses at the breakeven point. Typically the objective is enlargement of production capacities, extension of outlet markets or product differentiation. (Schefczyk 2006: 24, Bader 1996: 107, Leopold et al. 2003: 21 et sq.).
- *Bridge:* Is focused on financing in preparation for an initial public offering (IPO) or to overcome growth barriers before a sale to an industrial investor (Schefczyk 2006: 24, Bader 1996: 107 et sq., Leopold et al. 2003: 28).
- *Management buyout or buyin (MBO/MBI):* Financing of a business takeover by the incumbent (MBO) or an external (MBI) management. (Schefczyk 2006: 24, Bader 1996: 109, Leopold et al. 2003: 23 et sq).
- *Leveraged buyout (LBO):* Buyout of a business lead by a private equity investor. A LBO implies that the shareholding of the necessarily involved management is < 10 percent (Schefczyk 2006: 25, Leopold et al. 2003: 28).
- *Replacement:* Acquisition of equity positions of shareholders whishing to depart from the targeted business (e.g. founder or members of a family); no additional equity is injected (Schefczyk 2006: 25, Bader 1996: 108).
- *Turnaround:* This stage of investment is also often referred to as *restructuring.* Objective is to reposition the targeted business on a path of growth and make management adjustments; equity might be invested before or after restructuring (Schefczyk 2006: 25, Bader 1996: 108).

The first five stages can be associated chronologically with the life cycle model of a business. However, a chronological classification of the replacement- and turnaround stages is not feasible. These financing occasions might occur at any point in time in a business's life cycle (Schefczyk 2006: 25).

Figure 14 illustrates the different financing stages with their characteristic management challenges in the life cycle model of a business. The risk associated with individual financing stages shifts from being primarily unsystematic (business specific) to being primarily systematic (market specific). In principle, the level of risk associated with a private equity investment declines with increasing maturity of the targeted business. In particular, stage specific risks are left behind the more mature the business becomes. For example, a seed financing bears the risk of financing the development of unmarketable products as well as the risk of poor exit options. In contrast, the typical MBO only bears the risk of poor exit options without risks directly associated with product development. Accordingly, should a private equity investment pass through several stages, stage specific risks accumulate (cp. Bader 1996: 110).

Private equity financing stages

Financing stage	Early		Expansion	Late	
	Seed	Start-up		Bridge	MBO/MBI
Business stage	- Product concept - Market analysis - Development of fundamentals	- Business inception - Development toward start of production - Marketing concept	- Begin of production - Market entry or growth financing	- Preparation of - IPO - Sale to industrial investor	- Buyout from incumbent or external management
Profit/loss and risk expectation	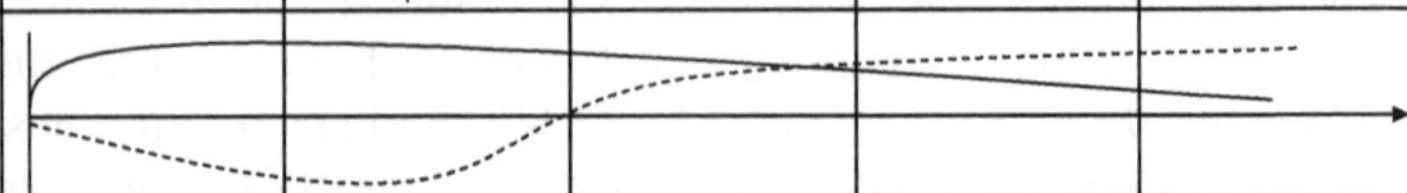				
Typical sources of financing	Private funds → Public sponsorship → ←		← ← Private equity	Debt financing Public market →	
Typical management challenges	- Assessment of product idea and market - Professionalism	- Distrust of investors - Search for management and other personnel	- Search for debt providers - Buildup of market position and image	- Increasing competition - Organizational challenges	- Financial strength of management - Dynamic of management team

Figure 14: Private equity financing stages. Source: Schefczyk 2006: 26.

The financing stages illustrate the different private equity financing occasions within the life cycle of a business. It appears that private equity offers appropriate financing in all phases of a business's life cycle. In addition, the stage specific demand for management support and typical management challenges are recognizable. For MBO and MBI transactions the financial strength and the cohesion of the management team are typically among the most pressing management challenges. Chapter 2.3.3 discusses buyouts in more detail.

2.3.2.2 Investment criteria, selection process and holding period

When screening potential investment targets institutional private equity investors seek to invest in businesses with a favourable risk-/return profile. Pivotal criterion is the expected return on investment. Return-oriented private equity investors are typically expecting a minimum investment return of 15 - 30 percent p.a., reflecting the yield on risk-free investments plus a premium for unsystematic risks, in particular (1) the default- and earnings risk, (2) the risk of capability gaps and the resulting need for advisory services and (3) the limited fungibility of the equity position (Leopold et al. 2003: 35-38). Further, businesses must match the specific investment approach of the investor with regard to stage and industry sector (e.g. start-up and IT sector). Also portfolio related objectives are relevant in order to minimize unsystematic (business specific) risks. Institutional private equity investors primarily seek to invest in those businesses which unsystematic risks show little correlation (Schefczyk 2007: 26).

The process of testing a business's suitability for a private equity financing is selective and time-intensive. Accordingly, this process typically lasts three to six months from the day contact is first established between an institutional private equity investor and a potential portfolio business until an investment is executed. Due to the specific and stringent investment criteria of institutional private equity investors only approximately 3 percent of all initial investment inquiries actually lead to an investment (Nathusius 2003: 386, Schefczyk 2006: 28).

Figure 15 illustrates the ideal type investment decision process in five steps. Guiding values for selection quotas in percent of potential investment projects reaching the subsequent step as well as essential selection mechanisms are assigned to each step (Schefczyk 2006: 27). The displayed selection quotas only have illustrative character and do not claim to be scientifically substantiated.

Ideal type investment decision process

STEP	TYPICAL SELECTION QUOTA	CONTENTS
1. Incoming business plan / investment proposal	100%	- Contact initiated by capital seeker or PE investor or referee - Initial screening assigned to investment manager, typically according to industry sector
2. Preliminary check of key data	25%	- Preliminary check of business (product, market, turnover, profitability etc.) and management on basis of business plan - Request for supplemental information
3. Due diligence	8%	- Personal contact with owner / entrepreneur and other key management, on-sight visits - Due diligence, typically in conjunction with external advisors such as legal, tax and strategy consultants, referees and industry associations - Typically issuance of letter of intend (LOI)
4. Investment negotiation	3%	- PE investor issues investment proposal (IP) - Negotiation of key components of term sheet - Valuation - Investment amount and degree of ownership - Financing instruments - Information and control rights
5. Execution of investment and subsequent activities		- Formal closing of participation agreement - Implementation of agreement (e. g. amendment of articles of association/partnership agreement, procurement of debt financing, management support)

Figure 15: Ideal type investment decision process.
Source: Author's illustration following Schefczyk 2006: 28, Nathusius 2003: 386.

From the perspective of private equity investment companies the investment decision process can be described as the search for equity-seeking businesses that fall within its preferred domain of stage and industry sector. The first step in this process is the acknowledgement of an incoming *business plan* respectively *investment proposal.* The initial contact might come about by a proactive approach by the prospective portfolio business or the private equity investment company or might be mediated by other private equity investment companies, banking institutions, external consultants or information exchanges. Documents received are assigned to a particular investment manager for screening purposes. During the *initial screening* the business plan/investment proposal is assessed on the basis of key data such as product, market, management and turnover-/earnings prospects. Supplemental information is typically requested at this stage. The bulk (approximately 75 percent) of business plans/investment proposals are turned down. Remaining investment proposals go into *due diligence* which typically requires affirmation of the private equity investment company's investment committee and/or management board. At this stage a first personal contact with the targeted business's owner or potentially a visit of the business's premises is common. The fit of the targeted business with the private equity investment company's investment criteria is often assessed in conjunction with external experts who, for example, obtain references of the business and the business's management, provide studies on the market the business is operating in or compile corporate- and tax analyses and recommendations. In this phase the private equity investment company places great emphasis on the business's track record. A proven track record is naturally a strong argument for a positive future of the business; in fact this argument is typically among the strongest in favour of a particular project (cp. Leopold et al. 2003: 122). In particular, the existence of audited annual financial statements (a) allow the private equity investment company to appropriately assess the targeted business's past performance thus enabling substantiated conclusions about the future potential of that business and (b) further signal the private equity investment company that a well-functioning accounting- and controlling system is in place.

Typically the commencement of the *due diligence* stage is preceded by signing a preliminary contract ("letter of intend (LOI)" or "termsheet") in which both parties ascertain the continuation of the investment decision process. After a positive completion of due diligence the private *investment negotiations* commence (approximately eight percent of potential portfolio businesses). Negotiations are typically initiated by the private equity investment company in form of an investment proposal. On the basis of this document, essential elements such as valuation of the business, degree of investment, financing instruments as well as information- and controlling rights are negotiated.[10] Very few (approximately three percent) of initially received business plans/investment proposals lead to *investment execution* and associated activities post investment. Here initially a formal investment contract is drafted and signed. Subsequently, individual aspects of the contract, e.g. modification of the business's partnership agreement due to entry of new shareholders or arrangement of new debt financing, are implemented. Now also the provision of management support to the portfolio business commences (Schefczyk 2006:28 et sq.). The holding period of the investment typically varies between two to ten years depending on the nature of the investment, the investor's approach and the exit environment.

2.3.2.3 Financing instruments

The choice of financing instruments in a private equity transaction is subject to the aspects of risk, control and earning potential of the targeted business. Under consideration of the individual conditions of the financing situation appropriate financing instruments are selected. These instruments ideally correspond with risk appetite of investors, minimize conflicts between management and investors as well as optimize incentive mechanisms. Further, the choice of financing instruments is subject to the financing phase of the business. In that way early stage investments are predominantly financed with equity instruments while later stage investments also make use of debt- and mezzanine instruments.

The most common financing instrument of institutional private equity investors is the direct equity participation which made 78 percent of gross investment in the German private equity market in 2006 (BVK 2007a: 9). 22 percent of gross investment was provided in form of dormant equity holdings, shareholder notes and mezzanine capital.

Later stage financings often exhibit buyout-typical financing structures (Nathusius/Bohm 2003: 438). These structures in a strict sense do not correspond with the private equity definition of this study since these structures presuppose the ability to lend against business assets. However, if one accepts that as part of the transaction new liable equity is invested in the targeted business, the fresh equity functions as leverage for additional debt. In this way banks typically advise debt seeking businesses to first broaden the equity base before negotiating on additional debt financing instruments (Nathusius 2003: 384 et seq.).

10 For valuation methods refer to Felden/Klaus 2003: 108 et sqq.

At the same time, the optimization of financing in later stage engagements is contingent on the purchasing price, the availability of assets to lend against and the estimated sustainable cashflow. Depending on the risk structure of the targeted business a senior debt portion (collateralized loans) of 60 - 70 percent for businesses associated with limited risk is typically recommended. For businesses associated with more risk this portion is reduced in correspondence with the non-existence of collateral. Further a mezzanine portion of 20 - 30 percent is common. According to the risk profile of the transaction the equity portion needs to be elevated; in no case should the equity portion amount to less than 10 percent of the total financing package (Nathusius/Bohm 2003: 438, Weber-Rey 2001: 504).

The author omits a rationale for these categorical dimensions. In this way these values simply serve as a means for orientation. The above outlined figures imply that sufficient collateral is available to make use of senior debt and that the targeted business exhibits a moderate risk profile that does not require an upgrade of the equity base. In this context it is important to note that a substantial portion of invested funds typically is not available to the targeted business. The rationale beyond this circumstance is that later stage, e.g. buyout investments, feature a transfer of funds to existing shareholders equivalent to the purchasing price of the business subject to the buyout.

2.3.2.4 Divestment

By definition a private equity financing is an equity participation over a limited period of time. Towards the end of the investment period, the private equity investment company seeks to "exit" and realize a return on its investment. The strategy for the exit is typically already decided and agreed on prior to investment. In order to work towards joint objectives and to avoid conflicts ex post it is essential that investors and receivers of equity capital have a clear perception of the method, the timing and the conditions of the exit when financing instruments are selected and contracts are drafted (Bovaird 1990:72).

According to many market participants the "ideal" exit route is the *IPO*. Correspondingly, an abundance of literature has been published around the IPO. However, only the best businesses are marketable at public exchanges. Further, the IPO is not only dependent on an optimal development of the portfolio business but also on a favourable stock market environment at the time of the IPO. Aggravating further are stringent regulatory requirements in many jurisdictions as is the case in Germany. The sum of these aspects makes the IPO much less frequent than other exit routes (Häupler 2001: 79, Schefczyk 2006: 38 et sq.)

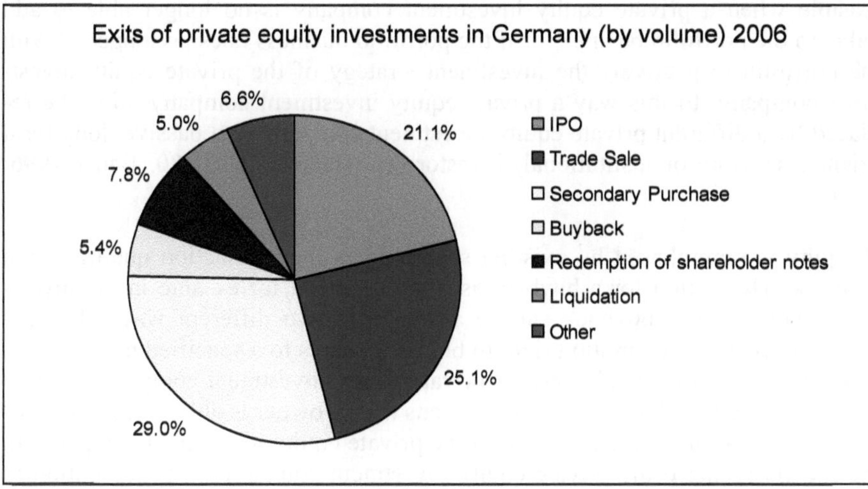

Figure 16: Exits of private equity investments in Germany. Source: BVK 2007a: 25.

The much more common *trade sale* is the divesture of an equity position to a strategic buyer. Buyers are typically competitors in the same industry (e.g. suppliers with the aim of forward integration or costumers with the aim of backward integration) or corporates seeking to diversify. For large corporates the acquisition of a smaller niche business is often a highly attractive option to find ground in a new market or to acquire technological know-how and entrepreneurial dynamic without much time expenditure (Häupler 2001: 80, Schefczyk 2006: 38 et sq.). The interesting aspect of this exit route is that a seller often is able to sell at a higher price compared to the price achievable with an IPO (Lorenz 1989: 129). One reason is that a strategic buyer familiar with a particular industry often is better able to recognize the "true" value of an investment. The second reason is that the strategic buyer generally follows long-term strategic motives, e.g. making use of existing marketing channels, other synergy effects and the access to exclusive know-how. Typically strategic investors take these factors into consideration while the general public does not. The third reason for a higher valuation is the control premium paid by the acquirer. While an IPO will typically result in a broad dispersion of shareholding, the trade sale typically allows for a controlling influence of the acquirer (Lorenz 1989: 129 et sqq.).

The sale of a private equity investment to another financial investor signifies a *secondary purchase*. While the trade sale often is a feasible opportunity for the portfolio business's management to divest their interests, the secondary sale is typically limited to the private equity investment company. A secondary sale is feasible when a private equity investment company is no longer able to add value to the portfolio business or if the portfolio business does no longer fit with the portfolio respectively the investment strategy of the private equity investment company. In this way a private equity investment company might be replaced by a different private equity investment company or a passive, long-term oriented (private or institutional) investor (cp. Häupler 2001: 80, Bader 1996: 147).

If equity is repurchased by existing shareholders the transaction qualifies as a *buyback*. The option for a buyback is often arranged for ex ante in the investment contract. The buyback can be arranged in two different ways: The co-owner receives a pre-emption right to buyback shares to a specified price. In this example the co-owner is buyer, the private equity investment company seller of a call option on the business. By this means the co-owner is able to (re)gain control over the business after the exit of the private equity investment company. In the second scenario the private equity investment company owns the option to sell its shareholding to the co-owner at a designated price. In this case the private equity investment company is seller and the co-owner buyer of a put option. In many transactions involving family businesses (including private equity backed succession buyouts) this appears to be the preferred choice of exit. However, a fundamental problem associated with buyback exit routes generally is the limited financial strength of co-owners (Häupler 2001: 81, Schefczyk 2006: 38 et sq.).

Finally, a *liquidation* will only then be a feasible exit route if the business is worth more "dead than alive". A liquidation can be contingent on bankruptcy or redemption of shares and typically conforms to a substantial or total loss of invested capital (Nathusius 2003: 389, Schefczyk 2006: 38).

2.3.2.5 Market structure

The private equity market is essentially composed of three constitutive groups. *First*, investors as capital providers, *second*, businesses as capital seekers and *third*, private equity investment companies as intermediaries. Next to these main actors external consultants such as M&A specialists, financial auditors and legal counsels are typically integrated in the process. In addition, banks providing debt financing are essential.

In principle, equity interests in private businesses might be acquired *directly* or *indirectly* via intermediaries. Typical motives for a direct investment are strategic- and cost related. However, the search- and screening capacities for the identification of potential investment targets, the standardized- and professional due diligence and the optimal planning of divestment argue in favour of an indirect engagement. This is offered by specialized financial intermediaries (cp. Nathusius 2003: 377), i.e. private equity investment companies. These intermediaries raise funds from a variety of institutional- and private investors and make these funds available to qualified businesses seeking equity financing.

Private equity investors in Germany differ tremendously with regard to investment approach. Businesses seeking funding therefore must closely review to what extend the business's objectives can be aligned with those of the private equity investor. This section will outline the sources of private equity and the motives of investors.

(1) Business angels: Business Angels are private investors that invest directly without intermediation. Provision of funds is often limited to TEUR 25 - 250. Particularly early stage businesses receive financing from business angels. These individuals are typically wealthy, retired entrepreneurs that not only invest equity capital but also provide management support and generate valuable business contacts out of their private and/or professional network. In distinction, passive business angels acting merely as financial investors are much less common (cp. Nathusius 2003: 377). The financing of succession by business angels is likely to be arranged only for small businesses. The reason is the high capital demand of larger businesses which a business angel typically is unable or unwilling to cover (cp. Nathusius 2003: 377).

(2) Corporate private equity investors: Many large non-financial corporates are direct private equity investors. Corporate investors typically target early stage and expansion stage businesses that have a distinct strategic attractiveness to them. This is particularly true for corporates that are not only seeking to invest funds, e.g. pension provisions, but are engaged in corporate venturing (Nathusius 2003: 379). Strategic objectives of corporate investors might be to (a) secure procurement and distribution channels, (b) access technology or products, (c) access critical resources such as research and development capacities or (d) spin-off business units. Only in rare cases the strategic objectives of the corporate investor are on par with return objectives (Nathusius 2003: 379, Schefczyk 2006: 20). Due to the focus on young businesses in specialized technology segments, corporate private equity is typically unsuitable to finance business succession (Nathusius 2003: 379).

(3) Captive private equity investment companies: Captive private equity investment companies are specialized affiliates or subsidiaries that are principally funded by a larger parent organization. Although third party money might be raised, the majority of funds come from a financial parent organization such as a

bank, asset management- and insurance company or public-/private pension fund. As is the case for non-captive private equity investment companies introduced subsequently, the provision of funds to portfolio companies typically occurs through investment vehicles in the legal form of limited partnerships. Similar to corporate investors, captive private equity investment companies often align their operations with specific objectives of the parent organization. However, captives are generally more return oriented than corporate investors (cp. Nathusius 2003: 262). In principal, captive private equity investment companies are able to finance succession in family businesses. Here, the financial expertise and the long investment horizon are quite attractive to successors (cp. Nathusius 2003: 380).

(4) Non-captive private equity investment companies: More than their captive counterparts, non-captive private equity investment companies are directly engaged in fund raising activities. As shown in figure 17, funds are raised from a variety of institutional- and private investors, bundled in a dedicated investment vehicle and invested in portfolio companies. Non-captive private equity investment companies are typically initiated by a team of experienced private equity managers. These managers determine the investment approach and drive fund raising activities. They typically administer several funds (concurrently) and pursue exclusively return-oriented objectives. In the German private equity market the approach of non-captive private equity investment companies has prevailed. For this reason this group is the dominating supplier of private equity capital in Germany (Nathusius 2003: 382, Schefczyk 2000: 78).

Providers of private equity capital can further be broadly differentiated between early stage and later stage investors of private equity (cp. 2.3.2.1). *Early stage oriented investors* primarily invest in businesses that are in a state of buildup or have recently started operations. *Later stage oriented investors* focus on financing profitable businesses that are seeking equity capital for various reasons, e.g. bridge financing to prepare for IPO or sale to an industrial investor. MBO/MBI transactions are executed by later stage-oriented investors (Schefczyk 2006: 9). If no distinctive early- or later stage focus is evident, the investor is said to take a universal approach. While business angels (1) and corporate private equity investors (2) invest directly and are typically oriented towards early stage investments, captive and non-captive private equity investment companies (3 and 4) are able to cover the whole spectrum of financing phases but will typically initiate investment vehicles dedicated to either early- or later stage investments.

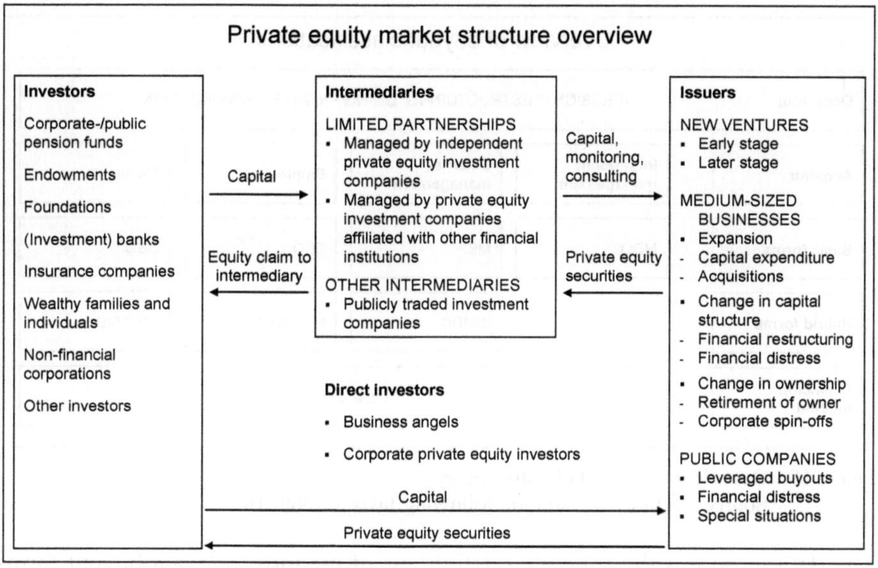

Figure 17: Private equity market structure overview.
Source: Author's illustration following Fenn et al. 1995: 4.

2.3.3 Private equity backed buyouts

A multitude of different definitions exist to confine buyout transactions. For a confinement it is important to note that the term "buyout" implies the takeover of a business. The term buyout is the source of different forms of buyouts that are denoted by added annotations such as management buyout, management buyin, leveraged buyout or succession buyout. Such annotations reveal the characteristics of the transaction such as specifying which party benefits from ownership transfer, classifying the financing structure or the occasion of the transaction. However, these terms might also be completely substituted by the term buyout which "... without add-on of additional explanatory term elements ... is not differentiable from a traditional business acquisition ..." (Vest 1995: 12). Nevertheless, the use of an illustrative characteristic appears useful for a precise and unambiguous wording and will be applied in this study whenever expedient. Figure 18 provides an overview of buyout classifications.

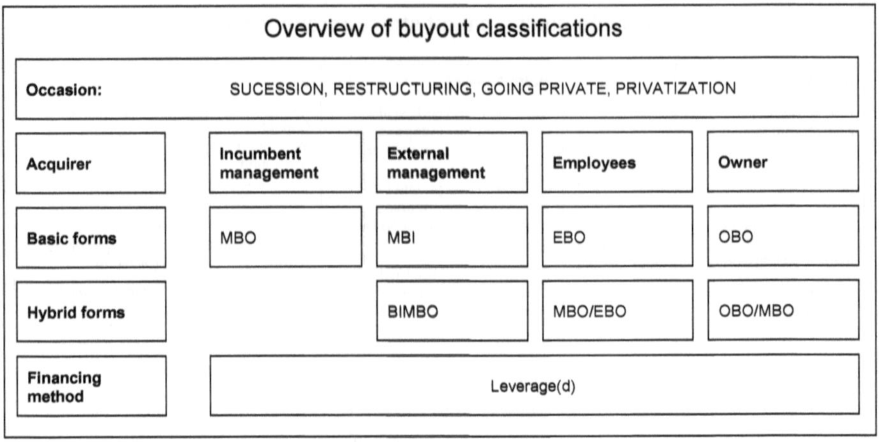

Figure 18: Overview of buyout classifications.
Source: Author's illustration following Jakoby 2000: 16.

The BVK proposes the following definitions of the most relevant buyout forms (BVK 2007b: 1):

- *Management buy-out (MBO)* is the takeover of a business by the incumbent management; the management holds in excess of 10 percent of shares in the business after the takeover.
- *Management buy-in (MBI)* is the takeover of a business by an external management; the management holds in excess of 10 percent of shares in the business after the takeover.
- *Leveraged buy-out (LBO)* is the majority acquisition by private equity investors; the management holds less than 10 percent of shares in the business.

In this study the author makes use of the definitions proposed by the BVK since they offer specific thresholds for the degree of buyout managers' equity participations in succession buyouts of medium-sized family businesses. Slightly misleading, however, is the BVK's nomenclature "LBO" due to its tendency to suggest that neither the MBO nor the MBI involves leverage, i.e. debt financing. In practice it must be assumed that the vast majority of such transactions make use of leverage. According to many authors in the field, the annotation "leverage" simply specifies the method of financing and does not allow conclusions about the type of acquirer (cp. figure 18). It can be assumed that the BVK chose the designation since on average a pronounced use of leverage in transactions led by institutional private equity investors is observable.

In the *MBO* ownership rights are acquired by an incumbent manager or a team of incumbent managers that change from a salaried to an ownership position within the targeted business (Spielmann 1994: 44, Huydts 1992: 20). Such transactions to achieve ownership succession have been practiced for a long time, especially in small businesses, before the term "MBO" occupied business life and academia (Huydts 1992: 15). A wide scope for pricing due to moral and personal reasons can lead to concessions on the side of the transferor with regard to purchasing price and payment method. "There are some owners, that demand the same price from their management as they would from any third party and there are some that downright give their business away" (Wiedmann 2002: 163). Advantages of the MBO can be compared to advantages of succession within the family, however the perpetuation of the family business ceases respectively is reorganized under the regime of a different family or families. At least, this form of succession preserves the cogent symbiosis of ownership and leadership (Huydts 1992. 14). Further, no business specific internals must be disclosed to third parties. The departing owner is able to withdraw quickly from operation since little orientation and no vocational adjustment is necessary. This advantage is shared by the buyout management team that should have intimate knowledge of the business subject to acquisition. The risk of finding "skeletons in the closet" ex post is almost barred in MBO scenarios (Wiedmann 2002:163). A buyout making use of the pooled resources of a larger group of employees (rather than the management only) is generally described as an employee buyout (EBO) (Achleitner/Fingerle 2003: 8).

The *MBI* is characterized by the divestment of ownership rights to an external manager or group of managers typically familiar with the specifics of the industry the targeted business is active in. This transaction differs from the MBO in that transferor and acquirer typically are not familiar with each other. Often MBI businesses have passed through difficult times economically and might have been subject to unsuccessful restructuring efforts in the past. In comparison with the MBO, the MBI must be characterized by less transparency concerning the business's economic situation and more resistance within the business towards change initiated by incoming management. At the same time, buyin managers typically are more prepared and able to initiate necessary change processes (Nathusius/Bohm 2003: 433). Generally, MBIs are associated with higher risk than MBOs. Likewise, the potential for value appreciation oftentimes also is higher for MBIs.

According to the BVK's definition, the distinctive feature of the *LBO* is that the vast majority (> 90 percent) of ownership rights is acquired by one or several institutional private equity investor(s) and that the initiative of the buyout is typically driven by that entity respectively entities. In particular, LBOs make use of substantial leverage (debt financing) and for this reason can also be regarded as a variety of a debt financed business acquisition (Leopold et al. 2003: 23). Main characteristic of all LBOs is the economic objective to concentrate the burden of the substantial debt financing (liability, debt service, repayment of debt, other economic risks) in the newly created holding company of the targeted business. In context of legal- and tax implications of such transactions, different risk profiles of private equity investment companies and involved buyout managers or differences in the ability and disposition to assume risk etc. should be considered (Holzapfel/Pöllath 2000: 226).

A common hybrid of the above introduced transactions is the *buyin management buyout* (BIMBO). Here the MBO appears in combination with a MBI and external manager (from the same or a related industry) join the incumbent management team. A BIMBO can often be advantageous due to the concourse of internal and external know-how with potentially synergetic effects (Wiedmann 2002: 165). It is important to note that in practice often a distinct differentiation between MBOs, MBIs and LBOs is not feasible.

Other varieties of buyouts such as the owner buyout (OBO), in which the existing owner remains a minority shareholder, are less common and are not focus of this research.

Chapter 2.2.1.2 highlighted the numeric overweight of succession buyins relative to succession buyouts in German family businesses. This might surprise since the MBI - in difference to the MBO - per definition brings a management into entrepreneurial stewardship that has no insight knowledge of the targeted business's operations, clients, suppliers etc. While an unbiased, fresh management start most likely is advantageous in turnaround-type situations, a lack of familiarity and insight knowledge can - at the same time - inhibit quick managerial success. However, among the premier reasons for the prevalence of MBIs in family businesses faced with succession appears to be the limited availability of qualified, non-family managers in these businesses. As will be discussed further in chapter 5, this phenomenon is very broadly explained by non-family manager's reservations towards family businesses due to issues circling around promotion prospects, independence and self-actualization.

2.3.4 German market for private equity backed buyouts

The private equity market in Germany generally is not as well established as in other European countries and in terms of capital invested is lagging behind the European average. In the last few years, invested capital in Germany was typically less than 15 percent of the additional capital invested in Europe (EVCA

2008). According to the EVCA private equity investments in Germany accounted for 0.31 percent of German GDP in 2007. Although this figure has steadily increased in recent years, Germany is still considerably lagging behind the European average (0.58 percent of GDP) and in particular countries such as Great Britain (1.69 percent of GDP), Sweden (1.26 percent of GDP), Netherlands (0.70 of GDP) and France (0.66 of GDP) (EVCA 2008).

In historic comparison buyouts for a long time had little relevance in the German private equity market. Since the year 2001, however, buyouts are the most investment intensive private equity segment, not only in Germany but also in other European countries and the United States. In 2003 and 2004 buyouts reached 71 percent of aggregate private equity investments (by volume) in Germany. Although this percentage declined to 58 percent in 2005, in 2006 the share of buyout investments in Germany again accounted for almost ¾ (72 percent) of all private equity investments in Germany (BVK 2007b: 2).

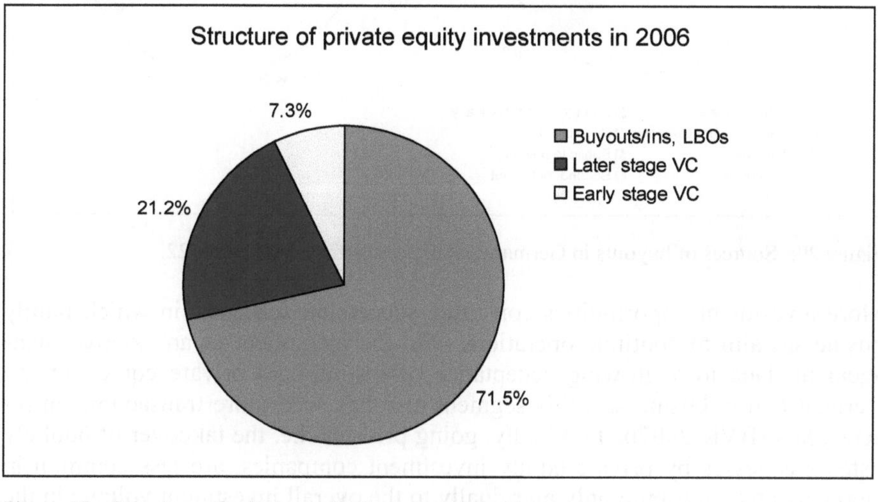

Figure 19: Structure of private equity investments in Germany.
Source: BVK 2007b: 2.

Since the turn of the century private equity investment companies focused on buyout transactions have made use of increasing opportunities for acquisitions, in particular acquisition of subsidiaries and non-core business units. Strategic investors have only recently been inclined to buy, so that private equity investment companies for a long time were regarded as preferred, financially potent buyers. Not only corporates have used buyout focused private equity investment companies to divest their subsidiaries, also private equity investment companies have sold a large number of portfolio businesses to other private equity investment companies (secondary buyouts). In particular since 2004 has the secondary segment seen a considerable upswing. Figure 20 displays sources of buyout investments in Germany over the last 10 years.

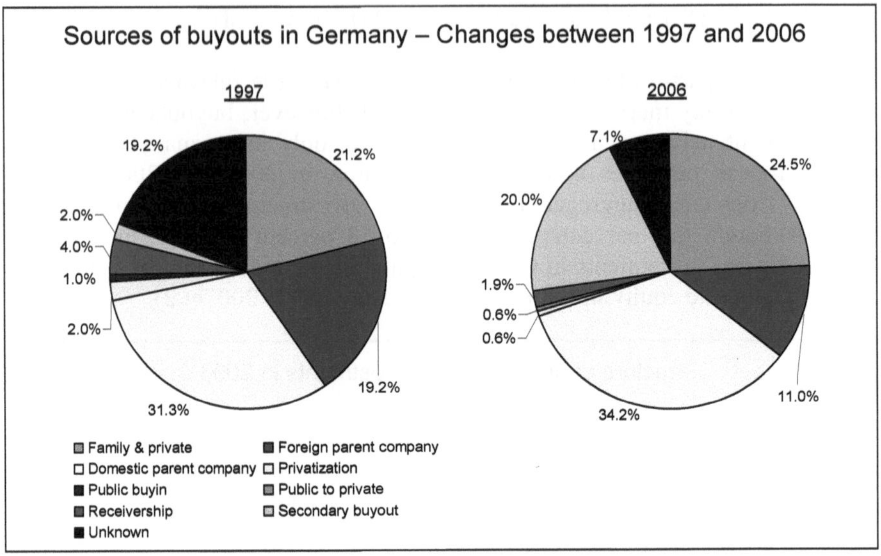

Figure 20: Sources of buyouts in Germany. Source: Schäfer/Fisher 2008: 22.

More investment opportunities constitute succession scenarios in which family businesses aim to continue operations with the incumbent or an external management. Due to a growing acceptance of institutional private equity among German family businesses, this segment also has seen more transactions in recent years (BVK 2007b: 1). Finally, going privates, i.e. the takeover of publicly listed businesses by private equity investment companies, are less common in Germany and contribute only marginally to the overall investment volume in the buyout segment.

Due to some large transactions aggregate buyout investments in 2006 reached EUR 2.6 billion and topped the 2005 volume of EUR 1.8 billion by almost 50 percent. However, according to the BVK, pivotal for this trend is also the persistently rising number of small and medium-sized transactions in recent years, e.g. in family businesses realizing succession (BVK 2007b: 2).

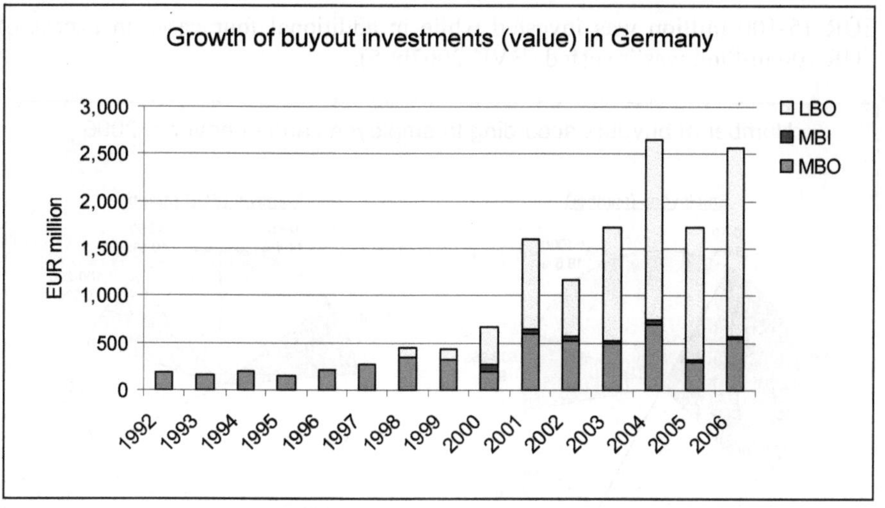

Figure 21: Growth of buyout investments in Germany. Source: BVK 2007b: 2

The BVK ascertained employment- and turnover data for 75 respectively 76 of 92 buyouts reported in 2006. The results of the BVK's analysis are displayed in figure 22. As in previous years, the emphasis was on businesses with more than 1.000 employees – 86 percent of all capital was invested in this category. However, with regard to number of investments the category of businesses with 20 to 99 employees was leading. Every second buyout was dealing with a business of this size. In that sense the structure of targeted businesses has not changed much in comparison to previous years although businesses with 200 to 499 employees have lost in weight to some extend (BVK 2007b: 4).

With regard to investment volume the most capital was invested in businesses with annual turnover in excess of EUR 500 million. More than 3/4 of funds were invested in this segment. However, most businesses that received buyout financing generated less than EUR 50 million in annual turnover. 2/3 of all reported buyouts in 2006 fall upon this group of businesses (BVK 2007b: 5).

With regard to size of investments, buyout-oriented private equity investment companies invested EUR 28.3 million on average in each portfolio business in 2006. This is an increase compared to 2005 (EUR 21.6 million) but less than average investment sizes in 2004 (EUR 44.8 million) and also 2003 (EUR 33.5 million). However, for 80 percent of transactions the investment size was less than EUR 15 million. In 14 buyout transactions reported to the BVK between

EUR 15-100 million was invested while in additional four cases in excess of EUR 100 million was invested (BVK 2007b: 5).

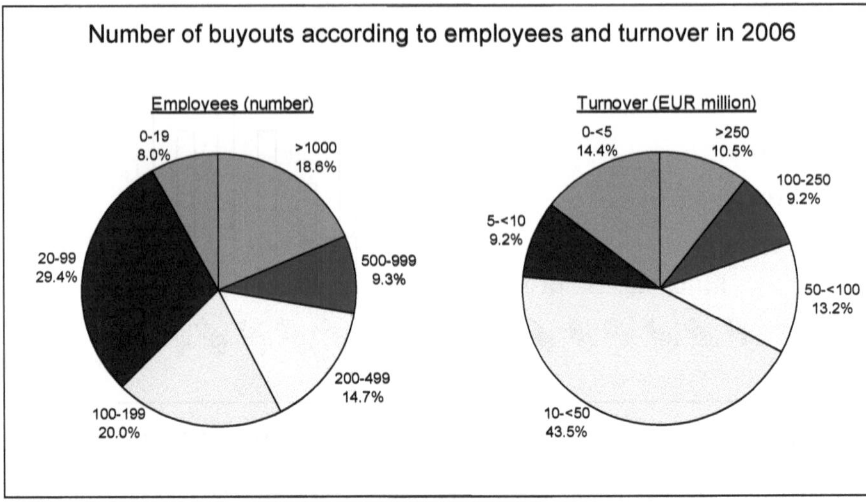

Figure 22: Buyouts according to size of target business. Source: BVK 2007b: 4.

2.4 Success factors

Central to this study are "critical success factors". For that reason an operationalization of the term is inevitable. The subsequent chapter shows that success is necessarily a relative parameter (chapter 2.4.1), provides an overview of the system theory perspective on success (chapter 2.4.2), specifies appraisal criteria for success in this study (2.4.3) and finally systematizes and operationalizes success factors (chapter 2.4.4).

2.4.1 Success as a relative parameter

It is readily apparent that "success" constitutes a relative value. While on one side it is necessary to consider the *perspective* from which success is assessed, on the other side it is necessary to consider the assessor's *objective(s)*. Generally, success is reflected in the achievement of objectives (cp. Bea/Haas 1995: 101). Therefore, the more complete the achievement of objectives of an individual, the higher the degree of success for that individual.

Contrary to the perspective of most authors (cp. Riedel 2000: 11, Weinländer 1998: 66) success in succession must not necessarily be equated with continuation of operation of the business after change of ownership (Olbrich 2003: 138). The assessment of success in succession must rather address the degree of achievement of individual objectives of involved parties. In this view also the borderline case of liquidation and thus the discontinuation of operations might constitute successful succession e.g. if the seller pursues a profit maximizing succession strategy and the liquidation of the business best serves this goal compared to other succession alternatives. In any case, it is conceivable that in liquidation scenarios individual assets of the business subject to liquidation, e.g. production sites, are integrated in particular value-added processes of the new owner(s) and thus resume operation.

In addition, in order to gauge success obviously the availability and ranking of *alternatives* needs to be considered. Success in its most elevated form occurs when no other alternative ranks higher among the assessor's preferences. The considerably challenging task for assessors in this context is to become acquainted with the full spectrum of alternatives. Further, it should be noted that the non-perception of alternatives ("bounded rationality") does not necessarily denote the non-existence of alternatives.

Preferences, however, not only differ according to perspective, they also *change over time* for several reasons. These reasons can be split in *self dependent* or *externally induced* reasons causing change in preferences. While the first group represents a change of preferences due to a change of personal attitudes, values, ideals etc. more or less detached from the environment, the latter represents a change of preferences directly induced by changes in environmental conditions on which preferences were constituted in the first place.

2.4.2 The system theory perspective

From a system theory perspective the safekeeping of survival of a system must be its premier goal. If survival is not assured, all other activities are superfluous. To Bussiek the safekeeping of survivability means stabilizing the system in an ever-changing environment (Bussiek 1996: 4). This can only be achieved in adequate adaptation to the environment and not against changes in the environment.

According to Niklas Luhmann, one of system theory's earliest and most prominent advocates, a system is defined by a boundary between itself and its environment, dividing it from an infinitely complex, or (colloquially) chaotic, exterior. The interior of the system is thus a zone of reduced complexity: Communication within a system operates by selecting only a limited amount of all information available outside. This process is also referred to as "reduction of complexity" (Luhmann 2004: 168 et sqq.). The criterion according to which information is selected and processed is meaning (in German, *Sinn*). According to Luhmann social systems operate by processing meaning. Furthermore, each system has a distinctive identity that is constantly reproduced in its communication and depends on what is considered meaningful and what is not. If a system fails to maintain that identity, it ceases to exist as a system and dissolves back into the environment it emerged from (Luhmann 2004: 288 et sqq.).

In this view a system is successful if it has the ability to adapt positively to a changing external environment. The objective then is to create a dynamic equilibrium between the external environment and the system (Ansoff/McDonnell 1990: 16 et sqq.). This ability for adoption should be anchored in the system structurally in order to remain functioning in periods of crisis. The preservation of adaptability appears to be of vital importance since it is the basis for survivability of the system. This implies that businesses – like any other organisms – are impelled to adapt to change in the external environment. Interestingly, this stands in contrast to the attitude of many business leaders that favour persistence on the status quo. As is the case for systems found in nature, unwillingness or inability to adapt to change in the external environment has life-threatening consequences.

From a system theory perspective then "success" essentially is constituted by nothing more than the survivability of the system. According to Gälweiler - under application of a system theory perspective - the premier objective of business owners should be assurance of survivability of the business: "... the sustainable, i.e. possibly long-range safeguarding of the survivability of the business" (Gälweiler 1990: 35). Schwaninger described survivability with the following words: "It is possible to speak of survivability if a system is able to maintain its identity, in other words a specific system configuration by itself is identifiable" (Schwaninger 1989: 183 et sq.).

This survivability by some authors is associated with positive growth since shear survival to them does not constitute success in a more narrow sense. In this context Bleicher adds to the criterion of "survivability" ("Überlebensfähigkeit") the criterion of "viability" ("Entwicklungsfähigkeit") and accentuates the aptitude of a business to arrange for preconditions of a qualified change towards a positive and meaningful existence (Bleicher 1994: 44). Survivability and viability thus is more than shear existence of a business but its existence in "prosperity and vitality" (Schwaninger 1989: 184 et sqq.).

However, the safeguarding of the survivability and viability of a system is not only measurable on the basis of hard facts but must entail soft factors as well. In context of business succession, questions regarding conformance with expectations of and claims by stakeholders of businesses to succession must also be considered.

2.4.3 Appraisal criteria for success in this study

As discussed in the preceding chapters the spectrum of perspectives from which to appraise success - and therefore the factors impacting on success - are necessarily diverse.

In SME research the manner in which particular objectives are developed and pinpointed is predominantly contingent on the owner's objectives. Appraisal criteria for success in succession from the perspective of the departing owner then are typically net monetary proceeds realized, the perpetuation of the business over a prolonged time horizon or the explicit expansion of business operations post retirement. Different, however, are the reasonable appraisal criteria for success on the side of private equity investment companies which are foremost concerned about the risk-adjusted return on investment. Next, for external parties providing consulting services to a succession process the volume of reoccurring mandates might constitute success while a buyout management team might be equally concerned with wealth accumulation and self-actualization. Finally, stakeholders such as a business's employees might aspire perpetuation and stability of the business subject to succession (cp. also chapter 2.4.1).

Considering the subjective character of objectives in the context of a research project that does not focus on one but several parties involved with the object of investigation, it is inevitable to determine common ground objectives applicable to all or most of these parties. In this study, the objective of *transaction closure* in a private equity backed succession buyout was identified to be a central, common ground objective of all parties principally involved in the process and thus ideally suited to be operationalized for success appraisal.

It is important to mention, however, that transaction success obviously only is realizable if other longer-term objectives of transaction partners appear to be attainable to a sufficient degree. In this respect, the perceived level of attainability of longer-term objectives certainly conditions the likelihood of transaction closure. Although a disconnection of "short-term" (i.e. transaction closure) and "longer-term" objectives of involved parties seems expedient for analytic purposes, in practice transaction closure necessarily is contingent on and reciprocally implicated by the likelihood of achievement of longer-term objectives of involved parties. However, considering further that unresolved succession poses a considerable threat to the survivability of the family business, completion of a succession buyout arguably constitutes success in its own right. This, in particular, holds true in cases of unstable, turnaround-type businesses constrained to realize succession in which the closure of a private equity backed buyout readily appears beneficial to all stakeholders of the affected business.

The author's central objective in this study is to identify factors with a distinct influence on the realization of a private equity backed succession buyout. The single and central criterion to appraise success in this study therefore is the completion ("closure") of the aforementioned transaction. On the occasion of transaction closure, ownership and controllership of the business subject to the buyout are passed to the acquirer(s). However, closure here should not constitute the fixing of an appointed date but rather the comprehensive transcription of legal acts (such as change of ownership rights, temporal restriction of withdrawal options, purchase price settlements etc.) coming into effect on that date (cp. Holzapfel/Pöllath 2000: 36).

Finally, it is important to understand that critical success factors can not be a standard set of attributes and measures. In line with the notion that the perception of success is rather intangible and subject to change over time, success factors equally can not be regarded as axiomatic. Critical success factors rather are the particular areas of major importance at a particular point in time. They must necessarily change as the business's environment changes, as the business's position within the environment changes or as particular problems or opportunities arise.

2.4.5 Systematization of success factors in this study

For the purpose of systematization, individual success factors might be bundled and attributed to higher-ranking "success potentials". Success potentials, then, can be understood to be systems of underlying success factors (Daschmann 1994: 5). For example, as chapter 5 will show, success factors associated with the success potential "private equity investment company" are "social compatibility and trustworthiness", "customized investment approach" etc. In detail, a success potential thus is characterized by the best possible specification of all success factors underlying the success potential. If all success factors that compose a success potential are existent in precise specification this circumstance might be referred to as success potential exhaustion (Daschmann 1994: 5). However, it is unrealistic to assume that situations constituting success potential exhaustion are frequently found in practice.

The effect of success factors then will be analyzed on grounds of the success potential on which they are constituted. For the examination of the relationship between success potentials and success factors the following is of interest: The association of success factors with a particular success potential, the strength of individual success factors on a particular success potential and the interaction of individual success factors among each other (*factual interdependency)* must be considered. In addition, the impact of individual success factors over time as well as the evolution of their relevance potentially is of importance (*time interdependency*) (cp. Daschmann 1994: 6).

In any case it can be ascertained that a very large number of variables affect success in a private equity backed succession process which, more over, are characterized by intricate cause-effect relationships. Due to the complexity of the research object owing to the number of variables and their interdependency in factual and temporal aspects, it is the author's objective to identify the *essential* respectively *critical* factors influencing transaction success. For that reason the analysis of success factors is limited to those factors that are considered to make a critical contribution to the realization of transaction success. In the search for critical success factors the author follows Daschmann and makes use of the functions of *selection* (selection and confinement of the essential variables) and *explication* (explanatory power of independent variables for the realization of success) (cp. Daschmann 1994: 12).

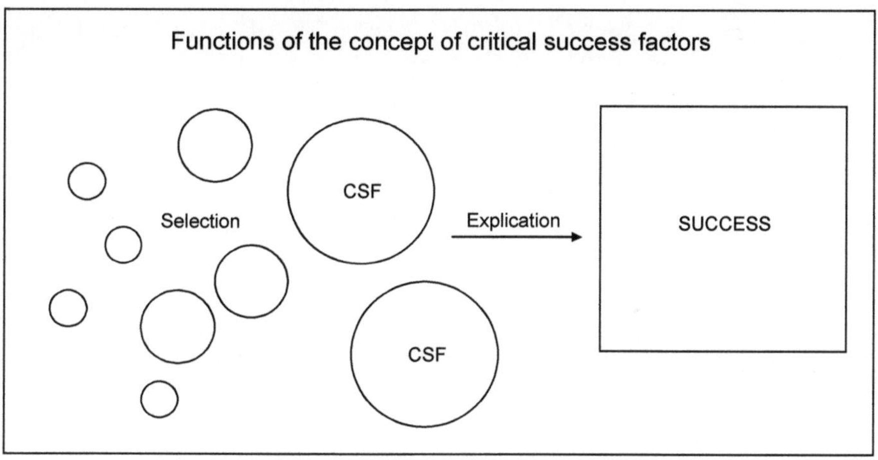

Figure 23: Functions of the concept of critical success factors.
Source: Author's illustration following Daschmann 1994: 12.

In order to reduce complexity of the research subject the author will systematically investigate success factors in private equity backed succession buyouts with the objective of identifying those factors that have a critical impact on transaction success.

3 Theoretical reference framework

This chapter focuses on the theoretical reference framework of the present study. The author chose to make use of Kern's interactions theory (chapter 3.1) since it appeared to provide a perfectly fitting framework for both data ascertainment and analysis. Subsequently, transaction cost theory is introduced (chapter 3.2) which provides insights to the functioning of the private equity market and which allows for a more substantiated analysis of process-related success factors in chapter 5.

3.1 Interaction theory

Kern's interaction theory builds the central point of reference for this study. Kern developed his interaction theory in 1990 from a number of interaction approaches in the context of industrial goods marketing (Kern 1990).

An early, relatively universal definition of interaction was originated by Homans: "When we refer to the fact that some unit of activity of one man follows, or ... is stimulated by some unit of activity of another ... then we are referring to interaction" (Homans 1950: 36). Since a business acquisition, such as a private equity backed succession buyout, always entails interaction between vendor and acquirer at the least, this theory builds an adequate frame for data ascertainment purposes and the structuring of data analysis. However, the present study forgoes to illustrate the exact derivation of Kern's theory by means of quoting primary sources. Only the theory's context with direct relevance for this study is discussed.

Kern finds fault that many interaction approaches only observe partial aspects of an interaction (Kern 1990:16 et sqq.). The overall context in these approaches is only insufficiently accounted for. Kern established three superior criteria that place the essential influencing factors in a collective context and allow for a systematization of fragmented explanatory approaches. These criteria are:

(1) Interaction partners: the seller-buyer relationship
Both the seller- and buyer side of the organizations involved in the interaction process - as well as the principally acting individuals - influence the transaction process lastingly. Organizations that can be characterized e.g. by size, market position or organizational structure, determine the frame of action of their representatives. This becomes particularly obvious when organizations have strongly formalized their decision-making in that they determine codes of practice and

scope of involvement for those individuals involved in the transaction process. Further, from an organizational perspective previously established business relationships between seller and buyer are of particular importance since they lead to a bonding that principally influences the decision-making. However, interaction behavior is always the behavior of individuals. This also holds true when they act on behalf of organizations. In that way the individual's characteristics and motives also need to be accounted for. "Matching studies" show that in particular the similarity of seller and buyer enhance the successful closing of a transaction process. By means of a congruent role behavior friction loss during the interaction is avoided (Kern 1990: 60 et sqq.).

(2) Sale situation: the framework conditions of the interaction
The interaction between involved parties can not be viewed in isolation of the external environment. The environment sets the frame for the complete process. The environmental conditions have an enduring effect on the form and breadth of the relationship(s) between interaction partners. In particular market features and cultural backgrounds of transaction partners might carry considerable weight. Further, the question whether or not transaction partners are dependent on each other due to the market structure (i.e. scope- and depth of market) will impact on the respective negotiation position. Finally, with increasing market dynamic the risk associated with the transaction is likely to rise both for the seller and the buyer and the behavior of interaction partners changes (Kern 1990: 58 et sqq.).

(3) Transaction process: process-related considerations of the transaction
The structural analysis of the seller-buyer relationship in a particular buying situation must be complemented by a process consideration which captures developments in the course of the transaction process. Only with the inclusion of this time dimension it is possible to incorporate the reciprocal interference of parties as the progression of action and reaction in the analysis. The behavior of interaction partners during the process is a central determinant in the process approaches towards interaction behavior. The content-wise focus of the interaction and the behavior of interaction partners determine the progression of the transaction process. In order to reach a detailed description of the interaction process it is therefore expedient to subdivide the transaction process in phases that are characterized by differing interaction behavior of the involved (Kern 1990: 63 et sqq.).

The use of transaction theory assures that all constitutive parts of the interaction in the research of private equity backed succession buyouts are incorporated. The three criteria introduced above provided a framework for the structuring of interview guidelines and main organization points in the analysis of data. In essence, this approach warrants a comprehensive reflection of the transaction.

3.2 Transaction cost theory

A comprehensive assessment of transaction cost effects of private equity financings is granted by the approaches of new institutional economics. Among these approaches are the property rights-, principal agent-, economic contract- and transaction cost theory. All explanatory approaches have common basic assumptions that are different from the approaches of neoclassical economics (Gutenberg 1976: 185, Weißenberger 1997: 135 et sqq).

Neoclassical versus institutional economics

Assumptions of neoclassical economics:	*Assumptions of new institutional economics:*
· market participants offer homogeneous products	· right of disposal is the fundamental attribute of goods
· market participants act according to the maximum principle	· bounded rationality of actors
· market participants react infinitely fast	· individual maximization of benefits of actors
· the market is perfectly transparent	· asymmetric information between actors
· preferences of market participants are suppressed	· institutional allocation processes feature norms and warranty elements

Table 5: Neoclassical versus new institutional economics.
Source: Author's illustration.

Under the premises of neoclassical economics exchange relationships between transacting parties can be settled without costs since all indicators of scarcity are reflected in the price of a product or service. Thus supply and demand can be perfectly matched. Contrary to markets in the neoclassical world the private equity market in the real world is characterized by frictional loss. Frictional loss occurs when the price of a product or service does not reflect all available information. This failure of perfect markets can be ascribed to the concurrence of bounded rationality due to uncertainty and opportunism of market participants. The assumption of bounded rationality implies that human beings strive to act rationally but are only partially successful in achieving this goal (Gutenberg 1976: 185). In particular this is attributable to uncertainty and complexity of the environment. The more uncertain and complex the environment the more difficult it will be for an individual to assess all possible information about a transaction. In this way, an individual is unable to judge if the price reflects all information.

Bounded rationality by itself would not be problematic if transaction partners would act altruistic. Then it could be assumed that prices reflect the information of the better informed party and as such are perfect. The assumption of opportunism however implies that human beings act opportunistically in that they strive to maximize personal benefit by exploiting a favourable information position and making use of malice and deceit (Williamson 1985: 47). In that way the price does not fully reflect all relevant information and transaction costs accrue. Thus transaction costs principally can be understood to be expenditures associated with the exchange of goods or services between two parties (Jost 2001: 10).

The transaction cost approach argues in favour of a relatively global thesis that transaction costs associated with economic activity are able to explain the existence of businesses and their organizational structure (Williamson 1985: 35-41). In this study, the transaction cost approach is used to provide a theoretical frame of analysis for the appraisal of private equity investment companies and the assessment of their investment activity.

3.2.1 Rationale for the existence of private equity investment companies

It is generally accepted that transaction costs occur when property rights are developed, allocated, transmitted and enforced. Financial transactions are characterized by costs associated with search for capital providers or -seekers respectively, information search- and provision costs as well as negotiation-, contract closing- and execution costs in substantial amounts. These costs are specific to the economic activity of realizing financial transactions (Williamson 1985: 15-42, Tietzel 1981: 211). Transaction costs, from the view of individual contract partners also *external costs*, principally make financial transactions more costly. In addition, costs that accrue prior to closure of a contract reduce chances of contracting since potential contract partners might turn away from the market due to these costs. In this way the transaction cost approach is in conflict with neoclassical financial theory that assumes perfect capital markets without transaction costs.

Financial intermediaries aim to reduce transaction costs that are the result of information asymmetries between contracting parties. Financial intermediaries are generally concerned with the production-, dealing- and mediation of financial contracts and financial services. However, from the perspective of transaction cost theory financial intermediation as a relevant form of financing activity is principally problematic. Due to the activation of intermediaries the transaction chain between capital provider and seeker is lengthened thus causing ceteris paribus additional transaction costs (cp. Hellwig 1991: 42). Considering the transaction cost approach financial intermediation then only is feasible if the advantages of intermediation sufficiently compensate the increase in transaction costs.

In literature different measures of financial intermediaries to reduce transaction costs are discussed that are also relevant to private equity investment companies (Benston/Smith 1976: 215 et sqq.):

(1) Institutionalization of search: Private equity investment companies constitute institutional meeting points in the capital market. The probability of contract closure in financial markets increases proportional with the number of contractors and their reasonable allocation to the individual market segments (cp. Gerke/Philipp 1985: 20-24). Since private equity investment companies increase choice in their sub-market with specific risk-, liquidity and redemption profiles, they contribute to the lowering of search costs and the augmentation of financing prospects.

(2) Provision of information: Private equity investment companies systematically collect information about potential portfolio businesses and utilize this information in the interest of a large number of investors to build their portfolio. Furthermore, in comparison to direct information search by investors, private equity investment companies are able to lower information search costs due to long-term business relationships, recognized discretion and trustworthiness as well as systematic management of information channels.

(3) Specialization: Next to search and supply of information private equity investment companies are specialized on negotiation-, closing- and implementation of contracts. They have detailed knowledge about the design of contractual relationships and command specialized personnel and systems to manage current investments. Due to economies of scope the specialization brings about the lowering of average costs per investment.

(4) Standardization: Private equity investment companies are able to standardize proven contract specifications and thus are able to diminish costs associated with negotiation and closing of contracts; standardized contract specifications are also able to reduce uncertainty with regard to appropriate constitution of terms.

(5) Optimization of lot sizes: Private equity investment companies are able to reduce fix costs of investments in portfolio businesses by making investments on behalf of a large group of investors. Investors would not be able - possibly due to budget or diversification reasons - to carry out comparable investments on their own. At the same time private equity investment companies are typically interested to work with a manageable number of large investors to minimize fixed costs associated with marketing and provision of information.

Consequently evidence exists that private equity investment companies generally have the capacity to compensate fixed costs associated with financial intermediation. If the activity of private equity investment companies is regarded as intermediation in imperfect markets, the assessment of the economic relevance of individual intermediaries must be as follows: A private equity investment company is useful, if the transaction costs associated with the intermediation are lower than the costs that would accrue without making use of a private equity investment company. As the case may be, additional benefits such as diversification or lot size effects must also be considered (Schefczyk 2006: 71). Thus the usefulness of financial intermediation in private equity markets overall is not provable. In reverse, merely the existence of a private equity investment company suggests that these organizations are better able to overcome the aforementioned market imperfections than individual investors.

3.2.3 Scope of transaction costs in the private equity market

Contractual relationships specific to the institutional private equity market are extremely complex. Schefczyk observes in particular three relationship levels (Schefczyk 2006: 61):

First, contractual relationships between *investors and private equity investment companies*, in particular the partnership agreement of the private equity investment company, govern the legal structure of the intermediary such as remuneration, conditions of (re)payment of capital and control rights. Second, contractual relationships in the *operational area of private equity investment companies* govern employer-employee relationships and the outsourcing of tasks with the help of agency contracts. At last, contractual relationships between *private equity investment companies and portfolio businesses*, in particular the articles of partnership with portfolio businesses, govern the structure of individual investments and - analogically to the first relationship level - in particular the (re)payment of capital and control rights.

The extent to which transaction costs occur is contingent on the design of such contractual relationships. A considerable impact on the extent of transaction costs have five different characteristics: (1) the specificity of the investment essential to the execution of the transaction, (2) the interdependency with other transactions, (3) the uncertainty due to environmental (external) influences, (4) the frequency of the transaction and (5) the measurability of value created (cp. Milgrom/Roberts 1992: 30 et sqq. and Jost 2001: 11 et sqq.). These attributes exert significant influence on the extent of transaction costs. While a strong value of the first three attributes generally increases transaction costs, a strong value of the latter two generally has a lowering effect on transaction costs. Thus every transaction produces costs contingent on the strength of the aforementioned attributes.

Since the study's research question makes a close investigation of the nature of the relationship between private equity investment companies and portfolio businesses indispensable, the subsequent chapter is exclusively concerned with transaction costs associated with contractual relationships between private equity investment companies and portfolio businesses.

3.2.4 Typology of transaction costs in private equity financing

In order to analyze different types of transaction costs occurring due to contractual relationships between private equity investment companies and prospective portfolio businesses, it is important to determine what in detail is attributable to transaction costs. The literature offers different proposals on how to structure transaction costs.

A principal classification of transaction costs is based on the moment of contract closure. Costs can accrue before and after contract closure (Williamson 1985: 20 et sq.). *Ex ante* transaction costs in this context for example are contract design and –negotiation while the extent of these costs significantly depends on the complexity of the contract. In principle these are the costs associated with the contract coming into existence. The control of rights and duties agreed upon and their enforcement are *ex post* transaction costs (Matthews 1996: 906). Assigned to the context of private equity investment the contract between a private equity investment company and a portfolio business differentiates between both types of costs. Transaction costs thus accrue prior execution of investment and post investment during the private equity investment company's holding phase of the portfolio business.

A more differentiated classification scheme is based on the delineation of transaction phases according to Picot (Picot 1982: 270). Here initiation-, negotiation-, control- and adjustment costs can be identified. The first two groups of transaction costs constitute ex ante costs while control- and adjustment costs accrue ex post. In this study the author differentiates between three phases that can be associated with a private equity investment company's investment in a portfolio business:

- *Initiation phase:* All costs related to the search, assessment and selection of potential contract partners are subsumed under initiation costs.
- *Negotiation phase*: Once a suitable contract partner is identified a contract must be negotiated and agreed on. Typically additional costs accrue due to the involvement of third parties e.g. lawyers, notaries and other consultants.
- *Holding phase*: Once the transfer of ownership rights and -duties is finalized each contract partner will control that the other adheres to the terms of the contract. Control- and adjustment costs that occur in this phase might lead to additional negotiation- and control costs.

At last, building on the notion that the economy is characterized by division of labor and exchange between economic agents, it is further possible to differentiate between *coordination-* and *motivation costs* (Milgrom/Roberts 1992: 29). The costs that accrue due to activities in connection with the division of labor and exchange of goods among different organizational participants must be organized in a way that warrants efficient coordination and flawless operations. The costs arising due to this coordination problem, e.g. the search of information or the exchange of information, are labelled *coordination costs*. A motivational problem arises if organizational participants follow individual objectives that are different to those of the organization. The participants thus must be persuaded to complete their tasks as intended. *Motivation costs* in this context for example accrue in form of control- or assessment costs.

A further categorization of transaction costs that accrue on the side of private equity investment companies and portfolio businesses in consequence of entering into a contractual relationship is proposed by Hack. Here five different types of costs are differentiated: costs associated with *(1) information sourcing, (2) information provision, (3) negotiation, (4) business- and relationship administration* as well as *(5) control- and adjustment activities* (Hack 2005: 124 et sq.). Information search costs (1) accrue when private equity investment companies screen the market for attractive investment targets and vice versa businesses seeking financing search for private equity investment companies that are able to satisfy specific (financing) needs. Subsequently, both the private equity investment company and the portfolio business are likely to have an interest in reducing prevailing information asymmetries and hence incur costs associated with providing information to the potential contract partner (2). Negotiation costs (3) occur when potential contract partners bargain over legally binding features of the business relationship such as information-, involvement-, and decision making rights. Post investment the private equity investment company faces costs associated with provision of non-monetary support to the portfolio business while the portfolio business incurs costs associated primarily with documenting adherence to contractual covenants (4). Finally, both the private equity investment company and the portfolio business incur costs associated with controlling adherence to contractual covenants and, potentially, costs associated with renegotiating such covenants (5).

The empirical part of this study (chapter 5) is exclusively concerned with factors that enable respectively inhibit transaction success constituted by closure of the buyout transaction. In the frame of transaction cost theory this implies the limitation of analysis to ex ante (coordination) costs for contracting parties. It can be derived that minimized coordination costs for contract partners must have a positive effect on contract closure i.e. transaction success. This notion is the starting point for the search of process-related success factors in private equity backed succession buyouts in chapter 5.3.

Figure 24 gives an overview of transaction costs and the classification in structuring frameworks advocated by different authors. Types of costs that do not have a direct relevance in context of this study's investigation (ex post transaction costs) are coloured grey.

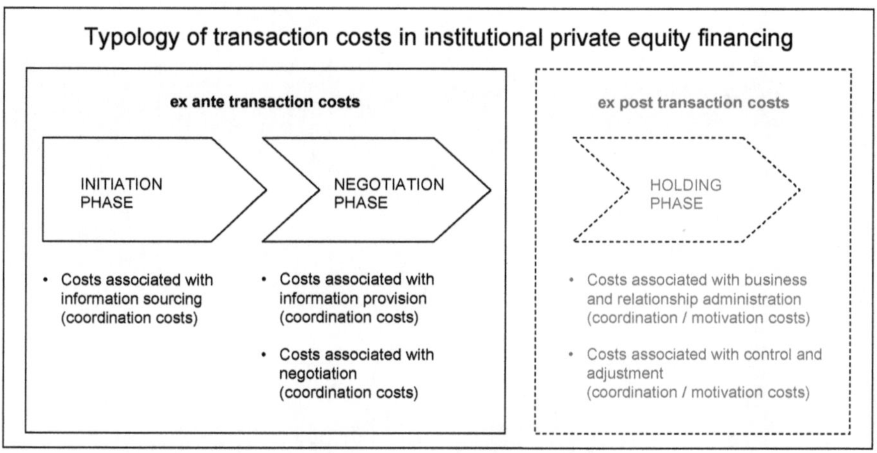

Figure 24: Typology of transaction costs in private equity financing.
Source: Author's illustration following Hack 2005: 125.

Overall, the transaction cost approach appears to be useful for the theoretical structuring of problems related to private equity financing but not deployable in standardized-quantitative research. It should have become obvious that in a perfect market, a market with no frictions such as transaction costs, financial intermediaries such as private equity investment companies would not exist. This chapter argued in favour of the existence of market imperfections and financial intermediaries in the real world. The existence of private equity investment companies was rationalized by highlighting how private equity investment companies are able to reduce transaction costs associated with direct private equity investment. In addition, this chapter offered a typology of transaction costs occurring in contractual relationships between private equity investment companies and portfolio businesses useful in the analysis and confinement of process-related success factors in private equity backed succession buyouts.

4 Empirical study

Chapter 4 is divided in two subchapters. Chapter 4.1 presents the rationale for the selected research method while chapter 4.2 in detail describes how empirical data was collected and analyzed.

4.1 Methodology

The overall research objective of this study is to contribute empirically to the understanding of private equity backed succession buyouts in medium-sized German family businesses. The study's central research question is formulated as follows: *What are the individual contributions of factors underlying the private equity backed succession buyout process and its success?* In addition, the purpose of this study is theory development rather than theory extension or theory testing. Therefore a decision was made not to prematurely prune the complex and multi-dimensional phenomenon of private equity backed succession buyouts into a shape that would fit within the constraints of a deductive methodology. In this respect the author follows Hamel who argued that "patterns of causality are extremely complex in most real-world administrative systems, traditional deductive-analytic methodologies force the researcher to declutter the phenomenon by (1) substituting crude proxies for difficult-to-measure determinants or outcomes; (2) assuming away some of the multidimensionality in causal relationships; and/or (3) narrowing the scope of research. In doing so, much of the potential value of the research is lost" (Hamel 1991: 84). A deep understanding of private equity backed succession buyouts in family businesses is a subtle, complex, and evolving process. Thus, traditional quantitative research methods cannot adequately reveal the underlying dimensions of factors contributing to success of such transactions. These considerations underline the necessity of utilizing an inductive methodology and suggest the use of a qualitative research strategy.

Common to all qualitative research approaches is that they seek to unpick how people construct the world around them, what they are doing or what is happening to them in terms that are meaningful and that offer rich insight. These research approaches represent "ways of meaning, which can be reconstructed and analyzed with different qualitative methods that allow the researcher to develop (more or less generalizable) models, typologies, theories as ways of describing and explaining social issues" (Kvale 2007: xi).

Research phases in the expansion of knowledge

QUALITATIVE PHASE	TRANSFER PHASE	QUANTITATIVE PHASE
Objective: Description and explanation of a situation respectively a phenomenon	**Objective:** Transfer from qualitative to quantitative modus	**Objective:** Testing of hypotheses
Process: Observation of cases	**Process:** Elaboration of consequences of first phase for the third phase	**Process:** Utilization of deductive statistics
Result: Description of general characteristics of cases respectively the situation	**Result:** Hypotheses for the phenomenon	**Result:** Affirmation, rejection or restatement of hypotheses

Figure 25: Research phases in the expansion of knowledge.
Source: Author's illustration following Cropley 2002: 52.

To Cropley the objective of qualitative research is to "expand the existent state of knowledge" (Cropley 2002: 49). For that reason a qualitative explorative research of the research object is necessary before deduced hypotheses can be tested quantitatively. In this context Cropley describes three phases in the expansion of knowledge: The first phase is the *qualitative phase* that aims to describe and explain a situation respectively phenomenon by means of observation. The second phase is the *transfer phase* in which a transfer from a qualitative to a quantitative modus is realized. This transfer occurs by means of formulation of hypotheses. Finally, the quantitative phase tests the formulated hypotheses quantitatively with the help of deductive statistics (Cropley 2002: 52). The research phases in the expansion of knowledge are illustrated in figure 25.

4.1.1 Interview research

In order to answer the study's central research question the author made use of an explorative interview research approach. Only by means of a qualitative analysis on basis of field reports the study satisfies the demands of the explorative character of the research question. Several reasons make the use of this research method appear most suitable. First, the limited amount of research conducted in the field of private equity backed succession buyouts in family businesses; second, the process character of the research question; and third, the sensibility of the topic for information providers.

(1) State of research: As highlighted in chapter 1.3, no empirical studies focused on factors critical to transaction success in private equity backed succession buyouts in German family businesses exist. Solely individual articles of practitioners on this specialized issue have been published to date. However, from these articles important aspects for the depiction of success factors in private equity backed buyouts from the perspective of financial investors could be extracted. In addition, these practitioner articles can serve as a reference in developing a basic understanding of the issue at hand and in constructing an interview questionnaire for the ascertainment of data. Since an empirical standard of knowledge with regard to success factors in private equity backed succession buyouts is not respectively only insufficiently existent, the prevailing state of research demands the extraction of such success factors and the identification of relevant interrelations among them. This objective demands a research methodology that is suitable to analyze the research object in an explorative manner.

(2) Process character of research question: The research question pertains to the complete private equity backed succession buyout process. This process consists of actions and interactions of the involved over time. Literature indicates that for research projects focusing on topics with high process character qualitative interview and case study methods appear to be more suitable than standardized (quantitative) methods of data collection (cp. Gephart 2004: 455, Yin 1994: 5 et sqq.). The relevant reasons for this are that standardized (quantitative) research methods are hardly able to depict complex processes in their entirety. Further, research methods for the analysis of complex processes should allow the researcher to pose additional inquiries and to utilize additional sources of information.

(3) Sensibility of research topic: Some authors suggest that sensible data is best collected in personal interviews. A study about private equity backed succession buyouts comprises necessarily much sensible data e.g. circumstances of succession, purchasing- respectively sales prices, sources of financing or other business internals that obviously are only disclosed reluctantly. In the context of problems for researchers to gain access to business internals Schmidt finds that "... businesses understandably do not have an interest in disclosing their strategic planning results and therewith associated problems in full detail" (Schmidt 2003: 140). Further, as is generally known "... for researchers the problem in practice is constituted foremost in observing strategy processes directly and retrieve information unfiltered at first hand" (Schmidt 2003: 144). In a personal interview, however, the researcher is able to build trust with the interviewee. In

making use of the personal interview research method the close interaction between researcher and interviewee is warranted and (a) even confidential data can be included in the research process, i.e. in particular in the phase of analysis and (b) interviewees can be assured that only authorized data in the end will be published. Due to the fact that family businesses in general are not obliged to disclose (financial) information, these business entities very often are difficult to gain access to. In particular, business owners typically have benign interest in sharing information about (their) succession issues.

4.1.2 Quality measures of the research method

Three tests were used to test the quality of the research method. These three design tests, namely objectivity, reliability and validity are commonly used to appraise the quality of empirical social research (e.g. cp. Kvale 2007: 120 et sqq.).

Objectivity: Since objectivity is a rather ambiguous term that goes beyond technical or conceptual concerns and raises epistemological questions of objectivity of knowledge (Kvale 2007: 120), here objectivity solely should pertain to "freedom of bias". Objectivity in the sense of "freedom of bias" refers to reliable knowledge, checked and controlled, undistorted by personal bias and prejudice. "Such a conception of objective as being free of bias implies doing good, solid, craftsman-like research, producing knowledge that has been systematically cross-checked and verified. In principal, a well-crafted interview can be an objective research method in the sense of being unbiased." (Kvale 2007: 121).

Reliability: Reliability pertains to the consistency and trustworthiness of research findings; it is often treated in relation to the issue of whether a finding is reproducible at other times and by other researchers (Kvale 2007: 122). This concerns whether interview subjects will change their answers during an interview and whether they will give different answers to different interviewers. Issues of reliability also arise in connection with transcription and analysis of interviews, pertaining to whether different transcribers and analyzers will derive at similar transcriptions and analyses. Therefore, the researcher's objective should be to minimize errors and biases in a study. "The general way of approaching the reliability problem is to make as many steps as operational and to conduct research as if someone were always looking over your shoulder" (Yin 1994: 37). In order to increase reliability of research findings interview recordings and interview protocols were used (cp. chapter 4.2.3).

Internal validity: Validity refers to the truth, the correctness and the strength of a statement. Validity in the social sciences pertains to the issue of whether a method investigates what it purports to investigate. Internal validity involves "establishing causal relationships as distinguished form spurious relationships" (Yin 1994: 33). Thus the research design should be able to determine whether event x leads to event y. In this study, two techniques were used to ensure internal validity, namely a reliable process of analyzing empirical data and enfolding existing literature. The interpretation of data and the formation of corresponding categories followed the prescription of the grounded theory approach (cp. Glaser/Strauss 1967). The comparison of results with existing, related literature has not only enhanced the author's confidence in the study's findings; additionally, the juxtaposition of existing results has lead to a more creative, frame-breaking mode of thinking.

External validity: If the findings of an interview study are judged to be reasonably reliable and valid, the question remains whether the results are primarily of local interest or whether they may be transferable to other situations and subjects. Critics typically argue that interview research offers a poor basis for generalizing results. Kvale responds that the consistent demand for social sciences to produce generalizable knowledge "may involve an assumption of a universal knowledge valid for all places and times, for all humankind from eternity to eternity" (Kvale 2007: 126). In his view it is rather practical not to ask whether an interview finding can be generalized globally, but weather the knowledge produced in a specific interview situation may be transferred to other relevant situations. "In postmodern conceptions of social science the goal of global generalization is replaced by a transferability of knowledge from one situation to another, taking into account the contextuality and heterogeneity of social knowledge" (Kvale 2007: 87). Further, the problem of generalization is not restricted to qualitative research in general or interview research in particular. "Whether or not statistics are used, inferences of generalization are always tentative. Data might offer confirming or disconfirming evidence, but never conclusive evidence. (…) The strength of evidence is a matter of judgement" (Kennedy 1979: 644). Kennedy emphasizes that "strength of external validity" or "strength of generalizability" would be a more appropriate term than external validity, because these terms suggest that generalization is a judgement of degree rather than binary decision.

4.2 Research design

Due to the complex structures of the object of research and the fact that private equity backed succession buyouts remains a largely unexplored research field a qualitative interview research method was chosen. This chapter specifies the sample of interviewees (4.2.1), the ascertainment of data (4.2.2) and measures used to analyze the data (4.2.3).

4.2.1 Sample

At first, the objective was to identify potential interview partners and contact them. Interview partners were sourced from four different groups in order to allow for a differentiated view on the subject and to include perspectives of all directly involved parties. Directly involved in the private equity backed succession buyout process are (a) family business owners, (b) institutional private equity investors, (c) buyout managers and (d) external consultants as well as other financial intermediaries. The integration of the different perspectives corresponds with the rationale of data triangulation. In that way a reflection and objectifying of statements of individual groups is aimed for.

Interview partners were identified with the help of databases and public sources such as company brochures and internet sites as data sources. Both professional- and private contacts of the author supplemented the access to interview partners. Central starting point for the identification of interview partners was the recent involvement in succession activities of a medium-sized German family business or the prospective involvement in such activity in the near future.

A further limitation of criteria for the selection of interview partners (e.g. selective consideration of buyouts only or buyouts that have occurred during a particular period of time or a similar parameter such as transaction size) does not appear feasible respectively might even be counterproductive since the objective is to identify the *typical* success factors in private equity backed succession buyouts. It must be assumed that representatives of all four groups - irrespective of the time of the transaction or the size of the targeted business - follow similar procedures and formulas for success in closing transactions. In order to capture *critical* success factors, a dispersion of transactions with regard to time and size is to be favoured. In addition, a limitation would lead to a considerable restriction of possible interview subjects and would make the operability of the study practically impossible.

To supplement insights from experts from these four groups, interviews were also conducted with two non-practitioners (i.e. academics) that appeared to be able to provide additional, valuable information due to their professional proximity to the research topic. Overall, statements of 18 interview partners are included in the sample.

4.2.2 Ascertainment of data

For the ascertainment of data semi-structured, guideline-oriented interviews, also referred to as semi-standardized interviews, were conducted. Bock finds that "... for the purpose of interviewing ... the design of a guideline is common, however its administration ranges between the strict adherence to written out questions and, on the other hand, the unstructured narration in context of a broadly defined topic. In the first case the interview is hardly differentiable from an interrogation and loses much of its qualitative function. In the later case a wealth of qualitative utilizable material is obtained, however at the cost of comparability of individual interviews, since interviewees rather than the interviewer is responsible for structuring the interviews. The semi-structured, guideline-oriented interview seeks to compromise between partially preset questions and the open narration, i.e. the flexible response to non-anticipated statements of interviewees in order to cover both reach as well as depth of the topic and to obtain multifaceted and comparable material" (Bock: 1992: 94).

The interview guideline used was developed under consideration of existing research and some pre-testing. For the structuring of the interview guideline Kern's interaction theory with its focus on the interaction partners, framework conditions and transaction process was utilized as a central frame of reference. Supplemental categories respectively dimensions were developed from existing literature or pre-test like discussions with interview partners. Over the course of the study the operationalization of factors determining success in private equity backed succession buyouts was continuously advanced and supplemented. Therefore the research approach can be labelled empirical and inductive (cp. Atteslander 2003: 36 et sqq.). By this means the author hopes to remain close to the social reality.

Although few questions for interviewees in groups (a), (b), (c) and (d) exactly matched, all four interview guidelines followed a similar pattern. All interviews covered six different sections with an aggregate of 16 questions for group (a), 19 questions for group (b), 17 questions for group (c), and 16 questions for group (d). Administered questions were split into two parts. The first part of questions (*market and environment)* intended to retrieve information about the experience level of the interview partner and trigger statements regarding market conditions for private equity investments in general and private equity backed succession buyouts in particular. The second part of questions (*transaction process and involved parties)* intended to trigger statements pertaining to the different phases of the private equity backed succession buyout process as well as the roles, motivations and behavioral patterns of parties participating in the process. At last, all interviewees were invited to point to neglected aspects of the research topic or add to aspects insufficiently covered in previous sections.

In order to allow interview candidates to prepare for the interview, the guideline was submitted to interview candidates prior to the conduct of interviews upon request. All interviews were conducted between April 2007 and May 2008.

4.2.3 Analysis of data

Data analysis consists of examining, categorizing, tabulating or otherwise re-combining evidence of an empirical study (Yin 1994: 5). However, "no standard method exists, no via regia, to arrive at essential meanings and deeper implications of what is said in an interview" (Kvale 2007: 103).

Nevertheless, some common approaches to the analysis of meaning in interviews – involving different technical procedures – do exist. In this study all interviews were evaluated within a qualitative content analysis.

Interviews were recorded and transcribed verbatim. In addition, notes to capture more subtle nuances of meaning and body-language expressions were taken during the interviews. Subsequent data analysis was based on interpretative methods in which key concepts and understandings are developed from the subjects' interpretations. The data analysis aimed to identify themes, consistencies or paradoxes. Interview transcripts were read and re-read to identify emerging themes. Transcripts were analyzed separately for each case by consideration of the research question. A running record of analysis and interpretation was kept, thus allowing the patterns of each case to emerge, before comparisons were made between cases.

Interviewees' responses were assigned to different categories and subsequently coded. The results of the analysis were systematically mapped and thereafter contrasted with the study's central research question. Since all interviews were conducted in German, citations of interview partners featured in chapter 5 were translated to the English language. The subsequent chapters will present the results of the data analysis.

5 Analysis and discussion

The analysis and discussion of results of the empirical study are subdivided into three cohesive chapters: the *involved parties* (5.1), the *framework conditions* (5.2) and the *transaction process* (5.3). According to the parameters of Kern's interaction theory each chapter evaluates factors essentially facilitating transaction success in private equity backed succession buyouts from a different perspective. With this approach the author hopes to stay close to the social reality.

The focus of analysis thereby is put on the directly involved. This emphasis accommodates the following circumstances. First, the qualities and characteristics of directly involved appear to have the most immediate effect on the success of private equity backed succession buyouts relative to other dimensions. Second, the author acknowledges that a detailed treatment of issues pertaining to environmental conditions would burst the scope of this study. Unsurprisingly, if any statements of interviewees with regard to the external environment could be triggered, comments were related to rather broad themes and rarely overly specific. Finally, a considerable amount of literature focusing on process-related issues of successful buyout transactions already exists. For that reason the author opted to analyze the transaction process from a transaction costs perspective which provides new insights to the research field and avoids the risk of merely reconfirming results of previous studies.

The arrangement of subchapters marks the relative importance of success factors discussed therein, i.e. more critical success factors were ranked higher in the sequence of analysis than less important ones.

5.1 Involved parties

This chapter focuses on success factors attributable to parties directly involved in private equity backed succession buyouts. Thereby the author undertook an exemplary assembly of participating parties that presumably must be extended or limited from case to case. Only if sufficiently frictionless interaction between the parties involved in a private equity backed succession buyout is warranted transaction success is realizable.

Next to directly involved participants – departing family business owners, institutional private equity investors acting on behalf of private equity investment companies and buyout managers – a number of specialized consultants and financial intermediaries contribute to a successful transaction process.

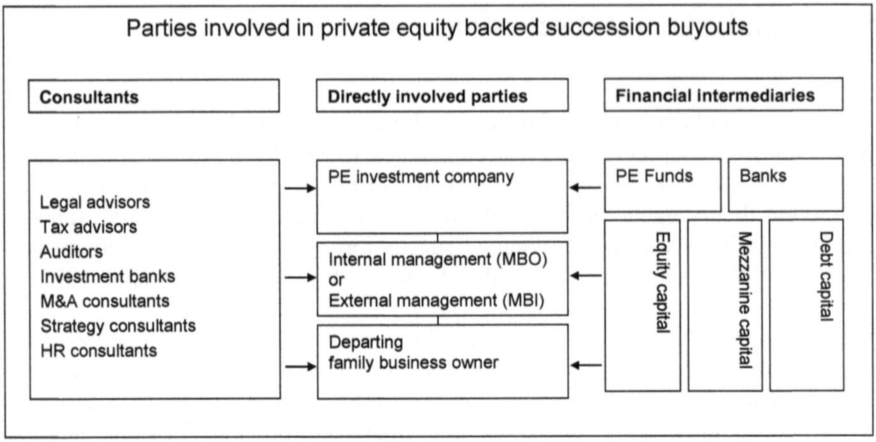

Figure 26: Parties involved in PE backed succession buyouts.
Source: Author's illustration.

5.1.1 Expectations towards family business owners

The following subchapters discuss expectations of institutional private equity investors, buyout managers and consultants towards family business owners that were identified to be critical to transaction success in private equity backed succession buyouts.

5.1.1.1 Attitude towards and experience with institutional private equity

In line with expectations a family business owner has towards a private equity investment company in terms of fit, institutional private equity investors necessarily expect their contract partners to have a sufficiently positive attitude towards their business model and business conduct. This possibly blatant aspect receives particular weight when considering the - to some extent - irreconcilable perspectives of institutional private equity investors and family business owners. While private equity investment companies necessarily are oriented on short-term, material objectives, family business owners typically are oriented on longer-term, often non-material objectives. This became apparent in the majority of conducted interviews. While the average institutional private equity investor's demeanour is characterized by factual sobriety, many family business owners often appear highly emotional when discussing matter concerning their business. This divergence is manifested in the different mind set of these parties.

Also Achleitner/Poech found that the difference in business cultures and the therewith associated ideals and norms lead to entirely different perceptions and behavior (Achleitner/Poech 2004: 4). While language and diction of family business owners oftentimes originate from sales- and technology backgrounds, institutional private equity investors mostly use terms out of the financial world. Further, while the family business owner's self-perception typically resembles that of the reputable tradesman not exclusively concerned with the bottom line, institutional private equity investors are easily perceived to be nothing but "controllers" for whom coherent financial figures are the sole indicator of success.

"The typical private equity investor and the typical family business owner speak different languages; different worlds clash." (Consultant)

Since all individuals seek a positive social identity and strive to differentiate themselves from other groups, prejudices serve as a means to borderline and appreciate the own group across from other groups and to safeguard one's own value system (Mummendey 1985: 185 et sq.). Other studies have shown that family businesses also refrain from making use of institutional private equity due to psychological barriers. Since family business owners are strongly attached to their businesses emotionally, some family business owners perceive the involvement of a private equity investment company as a personal defeat in form of a confession of the inability to preserve the business's independence. Since family business owners are used to be completely autonomous in their decision-making and to assume full responsibility for their decisions, the disposal of ownership rights signifies a massively experienced loss of control (cp. also Achleitner/Poech 2004: 3).

"With the participation [of a private equity investment company] we sacrifice the soul of our business." (Family business owner)

The divesture of a business constitutes a complex decision- and execution process and for this reason requires specific knowledge and experience. Thus oftentimes the skills required to identify situations in which a divesture via MBO or MBI constitutes a reasonable succession alternative are missing. In addition, often family business owners feel inhibited to formulate and implement a sales strategy. In view of the abundance of relevant questions related to the search for potential acquirers, the right sales- and negotiation approach danger of flawed decision-making on the side of the vendor exists, as also Jansen stresses (cp. Jansen 1986: 315). In the absence of the necessary strategic- and operative decision data the consequential information search and -processing expenditures can exhibit substantial barriers to a transaction (cp. also chapter 5.3).

Results of this study show that prior experience (ideally a formal business relationship) with a private equity investment company promptly increases the likelihood that family business owners consider a private equity backed succession buyout and are able to participate successfully in the divestment process, i.e. achieving transaction success. However, due to the considerable reservations of the average family business owner towards institutional private equity, prior first-hand experience with private equity investment companies typically is very limited. Aggravating the choice for a private equity backed succession buyout thus is insufficient knowledge about and experience with institutional private equity.

"We have little to do with the finance world ... besides annual bank talks and maintaining a good relationship with them this is nothing of importance to us ..." (Family business owner)

Previous research on the financing mix of German family businesses supports this notion and indicates that the dispersion of innovate forms of financing such as private equity is remote. Only less than 10 percent of German family businesses make use of private equity in their financing mix (Achleitner et al. 2008a: 28). Here the strong value of traditional financing instruments such as retained earnings and bank loans in combination with a perceived inadequacy of private equity for the business's financing needs make private equity appear unattractive to most family business owners. Along these lines two interviewed consultants confirmed the assumption that German family businesses in international comparison exhibit little capital market orientation in their choice of financing.

In summary, the average family business owner does *neither* bring the appropriate mind set *nor* sufficient experience along to make negotiations with an institutional private equity investor appear promising. The family business owner's lack of experience with institutional private equity considerably limits the likelihood of making a choice for a private equity backed succession buyout among other succession alternatives. Further, a stand-alone, unprejudiced consideration of institutional private equity often is not warranted, causing private equity backed succession buyouts not to be among aspired succession alternatives.

Prejudices that are reciprocally implicated by the external environment (cp. chapter 5.2.2.4) thus are likely to cause the average family business owner to brush off an approach by a private equity investment company (or an intermediating consultant) before a factual information exchange is possible. Elementary, prior experience with and a positive attitude towards institutional private equity were identified to be critical to achieving transaction success in private equity backed succession buyouts.

5.1.1.2 Resolute mind set

As highlighted in chapter 2.1, family business owners typically exhibit a high emotional bond to their businesses. Several interviewees from the group of family business owners indicated that letting go of their "life work" is one of the most difficult processes in their life. In contrast to large corporations that own a large pool of experience in divesting business units or subsidiaries due to an institutionalized acquisition- and divesture policy, the family business owner is unlikely to have had any previous experience in business divesture. In this sense, the sale of a business most likely constitutes a first- and one-time challenge for which the family business owner does not own any reference knowledge (cp. Bergamin 1995: 26).

"... Many private equity investors dread investments in succession situations since during the process often serious complications occur or even the whole process is abandoned. This is often caused by poor preparation of the process, non-existent financial figures and mood swings of the senior ..." (Consultant)

The dominance of the owner in family businesses was already highlighted. A disregard of behavioral science-, psychological- and social aspects in particular in divesture of family businesses would misconceive the specific situation pertaining to this group of businesses. Several factors then impact on the family business's decision-making ability and might cause a deferral of the divestment decision. From a process perspective the divestment decision itself can assume an almost indefinite time span. If no explicit necessity to divest exists, the process between the initial consideration of a sale to the final decision often is protracted. Findings in this study indicate that *perception barriers*, *emotional interdependence* and an *unwillingness to assume risk* inhibit the decision process and lead to a deferral of the divestment decision. Finally, the risk of protraction in case of a *dispersed ownership* structure exists.

Perception barriers in context of a divestment decision resemble stimulation impulses which are noticed by the family business owner but that do not directly lead to a divestment decision (cp. Bergamin 1995: 114). The lack of willingness to decide is closely dependent on the form and intensity of stimulation impulses as well as experience with comparable situations. In the case of business divestment these constraints are particularly pronounced: On one hand often no distinct indications in favour of divestment in succession exists; next to a number of relatively obvious reasons to divest this is another aspect characterized of haziness in which the senior is free to choose.[11] On the other hand the family business owner for the first time is confronted with a divestment decision. In the absence of comparison standards, decision-making models as well as personal experience, the family business owner often has difficulties opting for divestment – in particular if this is perceived to be the last resort in the succession process.

With the *bondage character* of earlier decisions and the voluntary commitment towards these decisions another inhibition threshold towards divestment exists (cp. Jansen 1986: 304 et sqq.).

"It is not easy to give away something one has been so successful with." (Family business owner)

Since the divestment is of fundamental importance and irreversible, the detachment from the once voluntary commitment towards the business typically constitutes a considerable challenge. The sense of responsibility towards employees, customers, suppliers and other stakeholders are likely to detract the family business owner repeatedly from a divestment decision. Expression of this responsibility is the "closure shock" which might manifest itself in the recession of the vendor close before contract signing (Baumüller 1988: 130). The widespread existence of behavior among family business owners characteristic of a „closure shock" was repeatedly confirmed by different interviewees from the group of institutional private equity investors. For that reason these investors expect family business owners to exhibit sufficient "preparedness to let go" or "disposition for disposal" when engaging in divestment negotiations. Consequently, the lower the family business owners "psychological ownership" of the business, the more likely is the commencement of the divestment process and, eventually, the realization of transaction success.

To a lesser extent this also seems to be true for the degree of the family business owner's embeddedness within the social environment.

"... the more a business owner is embedded within his or her community the less likely will be the senior's interest in a succession solution involving private equity." (Consultant)

As the quoted interviewee indicated, the reasons for this potential aspect of inhibition are likely to be caused or at least accentuated by prejudices towards insti-

11 This is particularly true in case potential family successors exist. Cp. also chapter 2.2.2.

tutional private equity widespread among family business owners (cp. chapter 5.2.2.4).

The perceived *risks* associated with the business sale further might be segmented into objective-intellectual and individual-emotional risks. The first group of risks manifest themselves in a "first-time risk", which can be ascribed to the circumstance that in the different phases of the divestment process as well as in the anticipated consequences of the divestment decision substantial uncertainty for the family business owner exists. The latter group manifests itself in a social risk, namely the danger of suffering from a loss of personal prestige and image due to the divestment decision. Jansen points to similar groups of risks associated with business divesture (cp. Jansen 1986: 291 et sqq. and 299 et sqq.).

Lastly, if more than one departing shareholder exist (*dispersed ownership*) and if multiple shareholders have authority to influence the decision, complications in the decision process proliferate. Here the antecedent persuasion of other shareholders of the divestment intension is necessary which usually emerges to be an extremely unsettling process as statements from interviewees confirmed.

Interviewees from the group of institutional private equity investors regard *initiative* of the family business owner to be a reliable indicator of his/her preparedness to divest. Concerning the initiation of the buyout process in family-owned businesses confronted with succession a previous study indicates that most commonly the vendor approaches an independent consultant (almost 30 percent of all cases) to initiate the sale of the family business (EVCA 2005: 13). In the same study the vendor approached a private equity investment company directly in 17 percent of cases and the management in 17 percent of cases. These results together indicate that the vendor assumes the most prominent role in initiating private equity backed succession transactions. On ground of these findings it can be argued that the initiative of the vendor to engage in a transaction process receives a high relevance in context of drawing conclusions about his/her personal preparedness to "let go". Initiative in form of a direct approach of the vendor signals decisiveness to potential acquirers.

In family businesses seeking a succession solution while needful of restructuring, an early disengagement of the owner appears beneficial and increases the likelihood of realizing a private equity backed succession solution. Here the family business owner may combine his/her retirement from operations pre divesture with the implementation of an interim-management that conceptualizes and executes potential restructuring measures. Also Mestwerdt found that a proactive decision of the family business owner to disengage from management prior to divesture may be beneficial in several dimensions (cp. Mestwerdt 1998: 200 et sqq.).

First, the business organization is able to break not only from old structures but also from a number of implicit elements of the previous basis of operations which are made up of the leadership-style of the hitherto existing owner. These must not necessarily have been disadvantageous or obstructive but they are extremely person-centric and largely leave the business together with the departing owner. *Second*, an interim management specialized on conceptualizing and implementing effective restructuring measures will be more likely to add value to the business than the senior likely to be substantially responsible for dissatisfying business performance. *Third*, the business will obviously become a more attractive acquisition target for investors, especially if implemented changes bear fruit quickly. By means of the deployment of an interim management employees may "practice" to deal with change that employees will necessarily be confronted with ex post. The specialized knowledge of dedicated interim managers with the preparation of the family business for sale can, in this constellation, effect that change does not lead to discontinuity in or a deterioration of business operations. This could be the case if the organization is not able to cope with implemented change and the quality of the product offerings, the market position and eventually the financial basis of the targeted business degenerates.

Finally, interviewees from the group of consultants stated that family business owners need to be able to accept that the strategic course of the business subject to the private equity backed buyout might considerably change ex post. Private equity investment companies typically make use of the exercise of various information-, codetermination- and control rights and substantially influence the course of their portfolio businesses. Only when a family business owner is willing to accept that an institutional private equity investor ex post will substantially influence the strategic direction (as well as economic well-being) of his/her business, a private equity backed succession buyout is realizable.

Although a resolute mind set might appear to be a most obvious condition for success and not distinctive to the private equity backed succession buyout process alone, the quality of the senior's psychological preparedness was found to be among the most critical factors in realizing transaction success.

5.1.1.3 Realistic price expectations and give-and-take disposition

A number of interviewees from the group of institutional private equity investors indicated that the purchase price to them is the most critical factor in the successful closing of a private equity backed succession buyout. This is understandable since a lower purchase price is appropriate to compensate for disadvantageous qualities of the targeted business. Accordingly, previous research empirically substantiated the high significance of all purchase price impacting constituents in transaction success (i.e. signing of the sales agreement) (cp. Jakoby 2000: 349).

At the same time, among other aspects, the assessment of the quality of a disinvestment for the family business owner occurs on the basis of the residual monetary value. This residual value corresponds to the value which remains after deduction of all taxes, management costs and consulting fees. High expectations of many family business owners with regard to divestment proceeds highlight the significance of financial barriers in context of the divestment decision (cp. Baumüller 1988: 129, Sewing 1992: 88). The initially claimed sale price often times is not based on substantiated evaluation but rather subjective emotional appraisal of the "real" value as well as the departing owner's future expenditures such as cost of living, retirement arrangements, provisions for family etc. which he/she seeks to finance with the sale proceeds.

"... Family business owners in most cases rate their family businesses much too high. This is often due to the ideal value that the family business owner attaches to the generation business ..." (Institutional private equity investor)

Institutional private equity investors repeatedly stated that price expectations of family business owners often times are unrealistic. At the same time family business owners often times are unaware of the fact that prices offered by financial investors tend to be lower than prices offered by strategic investors. While a strategic investor might be willing to pay a premium for expected synergy effects, most private equity investment companies will only pay a price that allows them to achieve their financial targets in a relatively short period of time (i.e. for example a money multiple > 2 within a time horizon of 3-5 years).

In order to come to an agreement the family business owner has to be sufficiently dedicated to close the transaction and at the same time willing and able to compromise. Unwillingness to compromise on price on the side of family business owners is constituted by statements such as the following:

"I told them the price I wanted and that was it. You know, I was not in the position that I had to sell really." (Family business owner)

However, compromising on price must not be an insurmountable problem as other statements of interviewed family business owners indicated. Other motives, such as business perpetuation, generally outweigh financial motives of family business owners. This assumption is supported by the observation that in many cases the business is sold to the prospective buyer with the most compelling acquisition concept overall.

"The concept of the buyer was just right for us." (Family business owner)

As previous research indicates, in more than half of succession incidences this is not the bidder offering the highest purchase price (cp. FAZ-Institute 2003: 19). The FAZ-Institute found that on average vendors are forced to accept a deviation of 20 to 30 percent of the initial price expectation when selling to non-family members in the course of succession (FAZ-Institute 2003: 23).

The strong emotional attachment of family business owners to their business might lead owners to deliberately withhold information that might depress the purchase price. However, eventually even-well concealed information is likely to come to surface in the course of the private equity investment company's due diligence process. Furthermore, the conduct during the due diligence phase might trigger quasi contractual liabilities. Although at the time of the due diligence no purchase contract has been closed, claims out of *culpa in contrahendo* may arise. In particular the seller may become liable for false disclosure and information with regard to essential facts concerning the business, e.g. financial status and profitability (Holzapfel/Pöllath 2000: 25). Severe cases of deliberate information concealment will most certainly lead to a breakup of negotiation talks as interviewees from the group of institutional private equity investors confirmed.

5.1.1.4 Participatory leadership style

The characteristics of family businesses respectively the activities of family businesses typically denote a paternalistic, owner-centric leadership style for which group decisions play a minor role. This proposition was also documented empirically in earlier studies. Bitzer found in his study 1977 that 23 out of 25 surveyed managing owners indicated that they decide by themselves even though in some points consultations or discussions with co-workers occur. Only two out of 25 managing owners mentioned that decisions are originated in team work and that the team assumes responsibility for decisions taken (Bitzer 1977: 100).

In the present study interviewees from the group of institutional private equity investors stated that the quality of the family business's leadership style has different implications for realizing a private equity backed succession buyout.

First, the strength and charisma of the senior might be such that the senior and the business make one unit that requires both to run effectively. In other words, the private equity investment company might be confronted with a situation to deliberate whether it can afford to invest in a business whose economic potential in the past was exclusively dependent on one individual. A large part of the value of the business is based on the business's association with the leadership of the departing owner and therefore is not transferable in case of an acquisition. For outsiders then it is difficult to assess whether or not the cashflow earned in the past is also achievable under different leadership. Although the retired owner might continue to serve the business (cp. chapter 5.1.1.5) during a transitional period, the succession motive presupposes his/her full retirement eventually.

Second, if the family business owner was following an unsystematic, non-participatory leadership style, it is unlikely that a second-line management was able to develop, much less able to assume leadership responsibility. If leadership responsibility in operative and strategic respects was exclusively assumed by the family business owner, fundamental principles of the viability and development potential of the business were most likely violated (Bergamin 1995: 39 et sq.). Such structural deficiencies in particular come to surface after execution of leadership change. If employees and managers were excluded from relevant decision-making and predominantly functioning as execution organs, they were unable to develop skills necessary to assume a leadership role within the business. Although a MBI might be a practicable solution in such cases, outside managers generally run the risk of putting those aspects of the family business's competitive advantage at stake that make the business an attractive investment target to the private equity investment company.

Lastly, paternalistic family business owners tend to be problematic for a third reason. An overly paternalistic family business owner simply is more likely to be a difficult negotiation partner than a less-paternalistic one and for that reason might easily hamper the transaction process. Emotionally charged and prolonged negotiations increase transaction costs for contracting parties (cp. chapter 5.3.3) and make transaction success more difficult to reach.

5.1.1.5 Ability and willingness to transfer knowledge

The majority of interviewees from the group of institutional private equity investors stated that the family business owner's ability and willingness to transfer (tacit) knowledge is important to the development of the business ex post. This is of particular relevance in cases of MBIs in well-run businesses without need of restructuring and/or strategic repositioning. However, businesses in need of restructuring are often better off with a "fresh start" represented by a new management that breaks with accustomed practices and rituals, as one interviewee from the group of institutional private equity investors specifically stated.

Contingent on the amount of proprietary knowledge "owned" by the family business owner indispensable to running business operations successfully it can be constituted that knowledge transfer from departing to incoming management is of critical importance to the success of the transaction process. The transfer of knowledge thereby is not restricted to the transaction process itself (ex ante) but also continuously occurs during a predefined transitional period after transaction closure (ex post).

In the course of MBIs in previously well-run businesses and especially when an entirely unencumbered management is taking reigns, the longer-term success of the buyout transaction substantially depends on the quality of knowledge transfer from old to new management. As discussed in earlier chapters, departing family business owners – irregardless of the succession route opted for – typically leave a considerable "vacuum" to be filled quickly and intelligently. If conditions for a sufficient transfer of knowledge between contracting partners ex ante and ex post are not warranted, the transaction is hampered early in the process.

The majority of interviewees from the group of institutional private equity investors confirmed that the transfer of knowledge ex post over a designated transition period in the form of temporary consultancy indentures, advisory board seats etc. should be aspired for and corresponding agreements should be included in the sales contract. However, at the same time, statements of interviewees indicated that demand for knowledge transfer by departing family business owners oftentimes is not met:

"The contribution of retired proprietors in advisory board capacities typically is less than initially hoped for." (Institutional private equity investor)

Findings indicate that ex post a free flow of information from old to new management is typically inhibited for two principal reasons: First, a large number of family business owners opting for non-family succession in combination with the divesture of all or at least the vast majority of shares have such personality that causes them to pursue a cut-off of all association with that business. Second, in particular retired family business owners with previously high emotional attachment to their business are likely to exhibit limited motivation in playing a part in that business's future due to their inability to influence relevant decision-making. This aspect, more than others, makes the prospect of involvement ex post overly unattractive to formerly authoritative, patriarchal family business owners.

"The opportunity to leverage on the knowledge of the senior is rarely there ... He [the retired family business owner] prefers a round of golf to sitting in the advisory board of a business he does not own anymore and which decisions he is unable to influence." (Institutional private equity investor)

In summary, the safeguarding of a sufficient level of knowledge transfer is critical to transaction success in cases of concentration of proprietary knowledge in the person of the departing family business owner. The question to what degree the departing owner is available for knowledge transfer ex post therefore must be part of discussions in the negotiation phase of the transaction process. However, despite the presumed importance of knowledge transfer for the viability of the targeted business ex post, the degree of knowledge transfer ex ante appears to have only limited direct implications on the likelihood of transaction closure.

5.1.1.6 Conclusion

Responses of institutional private equity investors, buyout managers and consultants indicate that these parties favour family business owners that exhibit the following characteristics: (1) appreciative attitude towards (and experience with) private equity investment companies, (2) resolute mind set, (3) give-and-take disposition, (4) participatory leadership style and (5) ability and willingness to transfer (tacit) knowledge.

Only if the departing family business owner is open to the mind set of institutional private equity investors and is holding a principal understanding of the functioning of private equity investment companies, a succession buyout involving institutional private equity is attainable. Thereby the acquirer's expectation towards the family business owner to be able to "let go" stands counter to the expectation towards the family business owner to stay involved ex post and transfer (tacit) knowledge to management assuming leadership.

The sale price of the buyout candidate business is pivotal to the decision-making process of the private equity investment company. If the price of the business for sale is sufficiently low, negative attributes are compensated and the targeted business still makes an attractive investment. However, several statements of interviewees made clear that if financial planning indicates that price expectations of the family business owner are unacceptably high, a financial investor quickly accepts that the project is unrealizable and terminates negotiation. Institutional private equity investors for that reason expect family business owners to have a realistic view on their business's market value.

5.1.2 Expectations towards private equity investment companies

The following subchapters discuss those expectations of family business owners, buyout managers and consultants towards private equity investment companies identified to be critical to transaction success.

Statements of interviewees elicited that private equity investment companies investing in German family businesses are confronted with a number of unique challenges. Compared with investments in non-family businesses the acquisition process is typically longsome and emotionally complex. Institutional private equity investors are expected to be appreciative of the targeted business's unique culture winning the trust of the owner with patience.

5.1.2.1 Social compatibility and trustworthiness

Social compatibility and trustworthiness were identified to be the most critical factors to family business owners when selecting among institutional private equity investors. The level of trust is of high relevance from the point potential contract partners start to exchange information. In particular during the due diligence phase of the private equity investment company confidentiality assurance is a highly sensitive issue. Since private businesses - unlike public businesses - have no obligation to disclose financial- or other information to outsiders, the release of sensitive data during the private equity investment company's due diligence process is typically a difficult step to take for the family business owner. A fundamental precondition for the family business's disposition to accept an in-depth due diligence including the release of sensitive data therefore is a sufficient level of mutual trust. In addition, the potential investor's intention to invest in the business must be sufficiently credible (cp. Koch/Wegmann 2002: 43 et sqq.). To win the trust of the family business owner and to signal sincere purchase intentions the private equity investment company issues a letter of intend (LOI) specifying terms of the due diligence process such as scope, duration and confidentiality assurance.

The high relevance of a trust-based relationship in all phases of the transaction process was repeatedly emphasized in different statements of interviewed family business owners. The paradox that lies at the heart of the issue of information exchange in context of a business acquisition is that the potential acquirer receives sufficient information to make a knowledgeable decision for or against investment and as little information as possible to prevent the business from harm should the transaction fail. For that reason family business owners seek to release the most sensitive information towards the end of the private equity investment company's due diligence process.

Family business owners emphasize social compatibility when selecting among private equity investment companies. This can be explained by the emotional and sometimes irrational constitution typical of many family business owners (cp. chapter 5.1.1.1). Family business owners are responsive to those institutional private equity investors that show respect for the owner's lifework, that appear sympathetic to his/her individual situation and personal objectives in organizing succession. As one interviewee from the group of institutional private equity investors observed, participation in social events such as "wining and dining" during the transaction phase can make the difference in winning or losing an investment mandate when pursuing investment opportunities in family businesses.

"The trust building towards the family business is the greatest challenge for the private equity investment company." (Family business owner)

"... For us the level of trust and sympathy was critical. If you give your lifework away to someone then it is not enough to make great contracts." (Family business owner)

These findings are supported by research on venture capital investments that show that the choice of the investor and the fit of the relationship between investor and start-up are important for cooperation ex post during the investment period (cp. Kuratko/Hodgetts 2004: 503).

As will be discussed in more detail in chapter 5.2.2.4 private equity investment companies continue to attract distrust in the German public. If at the time of first contact between the private equity investment company and the family business owner the investment company's representatives (un)knowingly live up to some of the widespread prejudices, further negotiations might be obstructed. This notion is accentuated in the comment of one succession consultant in particular:

"Private equity investors often have dollar signs in their eyes when they talk – with this I can't win family businesses." (Consultant)

The sale to a (group of) new shareholder(s) presupposes a high degree of mutual trust and "fit of chemistry" among contract partners. One retired family business owner explicitly stated:

"... The bottom line was not necessarily the sale price, it was the trust and the chemistry ...." (Family business owner)

Interviewed consultants stated that institutional private equity investors must cultivate their reputation like good private bankers emanating trustworthiness, reliability and discretion before anything else. The first impressions of the trustworthiness of the institutional private equity investor at the very start of the transaction process are likely to pre-determine aspects of the decision-making process difficult to alter ex post with measures aimed to improve the "climate" between potential contract partners. For that reasons Leopold states that the private equity investment company must place great value on the reliability of their management and the ability of their management to emanate integrity. A comprehensive preparation of detailed knowledge about the targeted business and a factual yet empathetic conduct of negotiations are essential to win the trust of a family business owner and substantially contribute to transaction success. Profound business experience and a noticeable high level of competence further supplement trust-building (cp. Leopold et al. 2003: 149).

One interview partner from the group of family business owners mentioned the high added value that family-owned private equity investment companies (such as the private equity investment organization EQT owned by Sweden's Wallenberg family) are able to offer. The favouritism of private equity investment companies with a strong family background, distinct tradition and a value-based investment approach indicate that these types of private equity investors seem to find high reception among family business owners.

5.1.2.2 Reputation, expertise and regional connectivity

The compatibility in core values and constitutional objectives of the family business owner, the institutional private equity investor and the team of buyout managers is of fundamental importance in realizing a private equity backed succession buyout. The family business owner's selection among potential acquirers is emotionally charged due to his/her strong personal attachment to the business, its employees and possibly other stakeholders. "Personal integrity" and "emotional responsibility" on the side of acquirers are attributes that play an eminent role as interviewees from the group of family business owners stated. From this it follows that a consensus regarding the business' objectives, principal strategic positioning and sense of responsibility towards the business' employees oftentimes are basic requirements on the side of family business owners before considering a private equity backed divestment decision. Closely attached to these issues are *reputation, expertise* and *regional connectivity* that constitute critical selection criteria among family business owners.

The high value attributed to the private equity investment company's *reputation* when opting for or against a private equity backed succession buyout became evident in different statements of interviewed family business owners, e.g.:

"... A private equity investor essentially must honour basic rules of entrepreneurial conduct. If we can not be sure about this we are not selling to them ..." (Family business owner)

It is generally accepted that private equity investment companies that are able to present a comprehensive track record of successfully realized transactions have a considerable advantage over less established private equity investment companies in sourcing new investment opportunities. Interviewees mentioned that a convincing track record essentially builds the private equity investment company's reputation in the market. This aspect in particular is illustrated by a statement of one interviewee with regard to the behavior a private equity investment company exhibited in auction processes:

"If you constantly offer too high prices and you are known to later depress prices then at one point you are not invited to bid anymore."[12] *(Consultant)*

This exemplifies that the reputation a private equity investment company "owns" in the market influences not only whether or not that investor is able to live up to expectations of family business owners but also to what extend that investor is approached with offers by M&A consultants, investment banks and other intermediaries in the first place.

Finally, findings in the realm of venture capital investors support the notion that a private equity investment company's reputation also has an effect on the performance of the targeted business ex post. In her study on post exit performance of portfolio businesses financed with venture capital Tykvova (2005: 22 et sqq.) found that especially foreign, independent and reputable venture capital investors are able to influence the performance of their portfolio businesses positively after an IPO.

12 In M&A auction processes financial investors make an approximate offer on the basis of an information memorandum and present a concept for the future development of the business. In conjunction with the vendor the auctioneer then chooses a number of candidates that subsequently engage in a full-fledged due diligence and negotiations with the vendor.

A number of interviewees from the consultants group expressed concerns about recent developments in the private equity market – especially among institutional private equity investors sponsoring large buyouts – with damaging effects for other market participants. These concerns especially circle around excesses in context of the early collection of "dividend-recaps", the charging of "consulting-fees" and the "overleveraging" of buyout financing structures. A continuative discussion around the implications of the cultural environment on realizing private equity backed succession buyouts in Germany is found in chapter 5.2.2.4.

In context of *expertise* the perceived certitude of transaction closure as well as the foreseeable speed of transaction closure are distinguishing factors influencing family business owner's decision-making when selecting among different private equity investment companies.

„High-ranking among selection criteria of potential acquirers is the associated degree of closure- and realization confidence." (Consultant)

Potential contract partners regard the private equity investment company's expertise as a reliable indicator of the investment company's ability to close transactions and - ex post - realize contractual agreements stipulated ex ante. In context of private equity backed succession buyouts these attributes allow the family business owner (and the buyout management team) to draw conclusions about the private equity investment company's ability to positively influence the transaction process and to add value to the targeted business ex post.

Some interviewees from the group of family business owners indicated that to them *regional connectivity* of the private equity investment company is a critical factor when selecting a financial partner in organizing a private equity backed succession buyout. For these respondents the national identity respectively regional rootedness of the private equity investment company is an elementary condition for building trust to the investor. The desire for regional connectivity also seems closely related to the expectation of a pronounced level of knowledge specific to the targeted business's market and operations.

"How can an investor sitting in New York understand my business, our products and our market?" (Family business owner)

Further, regionally embedded private equity investment companies also appear to better benefit from regional networks and references of local business owners (cp. Achleitner et al. 2008: 35). This can have motivational effects on the private equity investment company and potentially influences the transaction process positively.

5.1.2.3 Customized investment approach

Chapter 2.3 outlined classification schemes for institutional private equity investors along criteria such as size of investment, holding period, degree of ownership, industry focus or degree of involvement. Universally applicable criteria pertaining to an "ideal" investment approach of a private equity investment company seeking investment in a succession buyout are not identifiable. This insight accommodates the notion that a well-fitting investment approach principally satisfies the demands of each individual case. However, some common ground expectations towards private equity investment companies targeting succession buyouts in medium-sized family businesses could be elicited from interview partners.

Investment size: Ideally suited for the financing of succession buyouts in family businesses are private equity investment companies dedicated to finance transactions in the "small-" and "mid-cap" segments. Investment sizes in these segments may range between EUR 0.5 - 100 million and typically target businesses with annual turnover between EUR 10 - 500 million. Most "large-cap", buyout focused private equity investors today do not target family businesses and rather invest in "carve-out" or "spin-off" transactions that easily exceed the investment sizes that the majority of family-owned businesses are able to satisfy. In other words, for these investors most family businesses are much too small to make interesting investment targets.

Investment horizon: The circumstance that private equity investment companies per definition are only "partners over time" was found to be among the most commonly mentioned reasons why family business owners would not consider a private equity backed succession buyout to organize succession. Unsurprisingly, the majority of equity capital seekers are interested in a lasting financing (cp. Arnold 1989: 211-217). In this context one family business owner commented:

"The short-sightedness of private equity investors runs diametric to the long-term orientation of the typical family business". (Family business owner)

Although this statement was made in abstraction of succession, it signifies the deep-rooted reservations of many family business owners towards private equity investment companies due to their short investment horizon. As already discussed, the limited investment horizon jeopardizes the typical vendor's objective to opt for a sustainable succession solution promising long-term perpetuation of his/her business. In context of private equity sponsored succession buyouts the short-term orientation of many private equity investment companies also runs counter to the presumably long-term objectives of buyout managers and their entrepreneurial ambitions (cp. chapter 5.1.3.4). At the time of the private equity investment company's exit changes in the affected business's shareholder structure are inevitable constituting a threat to business perpetuation. For that reason ex ante both the family business owner and buyout managers will deliberate about the private equity investor's investment horizon, including possible and aspired exit routes.

The myopia of private equity investment companies can be attributed to different rationales. In order to reduce information problems (information asymmetry) between the private equity investment company and the portfolio business, the private equity investor limits the investment period to a few years only. Further, the private equity investment company is compelled to satisfy return expectations of investors and thus must generate an adequate return over a preferably short period of time. Since the business model of private equity investment companies is not geared towards recurring dividend distributions of portfolio businesses, the investor's rate of return is principally contingent on divesting portfolio businesses at a premium to purchase prices ("exit-orientation"). Quick exit success for the private equity investment company especially is important if the investment company intends to engage in fundraising activities for the opening of a new investment vehicle and does not yet own a meaningful track record (cp. Tykvova 2005: 15). However, since the value enhancement phase ex post for previously family-owned businesses often tends to be longer than for other types of businesses, the private equity investment company's holding period for a previously family-owned business also tends to be longer than the holding period for other types of businesses. One interviewee from the group of institutional private equity investment companies particularly mentioned that the average holding period for their portfolio of previously family-owned businesses outlives the holding period for other, not previously family-owned portfolio business (4-5 years vs. 3-4 years).

Interviewees from the group of buyout managers indicated that they have a preference towards redemption rights as long as these are not exclusively executable by the private equity investment company. Typically redemption rights in form of early re-purchase rights ("right of first refusal") are aspired (cp. Leopold 2003: 100). Further, redemption rights are frequently bound to substantial redemption periods and partially to the existence of pre-defined occasions to redeem shares (cp. Schefczyk 2006: 22).

Degree of ownership: As discussed in chapter 2.3.1 buyouts are characterized by the acquisition of all or at least the majority of equity (ownership rights) in the targeted business. Considering further the scope of transaction sizes and the limited capital resources of the average buyout manager it becomes obvious that a private equity backed succession buyout falls within the investment range of private equity investment companies dedicated to majority investments.

Knowledge of business and industry: The private equity investment company typically is expected to have a detailed understanding of both the family business's operations and the market the family business is active in, according to an interviewee in the group of family business owners. This has considerable weight for both the departing family business owner and buyout managers seeking not only a financial partner but one with detailed knowledge of the business's operations and market(s). This expectation towards a private equity investment company is exemplified by one interviewee's expression in particular:

"... A private equity investor? They don't understand our business ..." (Family business owner)

It can be constituted that both family business owners and buyout managers favour private equity investment companies with a dedicated industry focus when selecting among institutional private equity investors to realize a private equity backed succession buyout.

Contributions to the transaction process: Statements of interviewed buyout managers pointed to contributions to the buyout transaction process expected of institutional private equity investors. Here respondents in particular mentioned support in structuring the acquisition financing and negotiating the purchase price. The findings are generally supported by a previous empirical study on family businesses that have realized succession via a private equity sponsored buyout indicating that the most important contribution to the buyout process lies in structuring the finance, second, in shaping the due diligence process, followed by the private equity investment company's contribution to negotiating the business' valuation with the vendor (EVCA 2005: 14).

Capacity to add value ex post: Generally both the family business owner and buyout managers favour private equity investment companies that own or are able to acquire detailed knowledge about the targeted business's operating processes. Especially buyout managers favour private equity investment companies that are able to contribute to a review and refinement of these processes if need be. Past studies identified evaluation of potential market growth followed by assessment of existing management and assistance in suggesting new management to be among the most sought-after contributions of private equity investment companies to portfolio businesses during the investment period (cp. EVCA 2005: 14 et sq.). In the same study respondents appreciated that private equity investment companies conduct recurring strategic reviews and, in businesses in need of turnaround, suggest restructuring measures and strategic repositioning.

5.1.2.4 Involvement and scope of influence

Involvement of the private equity investment company in the transaction process ex ante was principally regarded as favourable from all groups of interviewees.

"I know cases in which the private equity investor was holding together the whole process ... They [representatives of the private equity investment company] were following something like an appeasement strategy because the vendor and the management did not communicate well." (Consultant)

In a private equity backed succession buyout/-in the private equity investment company necessarily is closely involved in all phases of the transaction process. As outside (co)investors they are not only able to support buyout managers in different phases of the acquisition process, they might also function as a fairly neutral partner able to lead negotiations with the vendor in conflict-free terrain. This aspect in particular can be of particular relevance in MBO transactions where the vendor remains the employer for acquiring managers until a sale agreement is coming into effect and where negotiations might be especially emotional.

As already discussed in chapter 2.3.2, private equity investment companies continue to stay involved in their portfolio businesses ex post. Private equity investment companies typically seek to add value to their portfolio businesses by making use of their information- and codetermination rights thereby seeking to influence the course of the targeted business in all matters of strategic relevance. In addition, activities such as identifying and retaining capable management and other personnel, support of marketing activities, establishment of contacts to business partners, risk management and general consulting are generally attributed to private equity investment companies. However, to what degree this is actually realized in practice is subject to controversial discussion in academia (cp. Schefczyk 2000: 23). The analysis of interviews within the scope of this study led to a similar, inconclusive picture.

Schefczyk differentiates between three levels of codetermination- and counselling intensiveness. *First*, this is a limited involvement in governing bodies of the business (advisory- and supervisory board etc.) which can be labelled as counselling in a broader sense. According to Schefczyk, this type of involvement is observable in the vast majority (87 percent) of all investments sponsored by institutional private equity investors. The objective here is to minimize total losses. The *second* level of involvement is characteristic of an active patronage of day-to-day business administration which can be labelled as counselling in a more narrow sense. Schefzyk observes that this level of involvement occurs in almost half (42 percent) of all investments backed by institutional private equity. The objective of investors in this context is the cut of losses by exercising information- and control rights. Further, the private equity investor's objective is performance enhancement by means of enhanced involvement. *Third*, in rare occasions private equity investors might temporarily assume operative line assignments in their portfolio businesses. However, this level of involvement is observable in only approximately 10 percent of all investments pursued by private equity investment companies (Schefczyk 2000: 133 / 142).

In the context of business succession and the apprehension of successors that a private equity investment company might overly interfere in day-to-day management decisions or decisions of strategic importance, questions were asked to interviewees about the aspired scope of the private equity investment company's involvement and expected level of consultancy support. Interviewees from the group of buyout managers indicated that they seek to be as free as possible in decision-making pertaining to day-to-day business operations. Codetermination and counselling in the most pronounced form clearly is not expected and - for that reason - typically not practiced in buyout transactions. However, support clearly is sought in all aspects related to financing. Schefczyk's results confirm that the emphasis of private equity investment companies' contributions in practice often are circling around issues of financing. In difference to early stage investments the private equity investment company's involvement in later stage transactions is typically limited to the exercise of information- and control rights without any active involvement in day-to-day business administration. As became clear from interviews, in case of MBO/MBI transactions institutional private equity investment companies particularly invest in the new management team of a targeted business. This typically allows for restraint from counselling and codetermination in a more narrow sense (Schefczyk 2000: 143 et sq.).

Results confirm that departing owners and successors equally expect involvement of a private equity investment company ex post (in businesses subject to a private equity sponsored succession buyout) to be moderate only. If the private equity investment company's degree of control is clearly defined ex ante and information about the prospective manner of involvement shared freely among contract partners, exercise of control and involvement per se were not found to be objectionable to neither family business owners nor buyout managers.

In summary, the level of involvement and scope of influence of the private equity investment company ex post were found to be neither a deal maker nor a deal breaker. This might be attributable to the somewhat unemotional view expressed in interviews that the sheer involvement of the private equity investment company in governmental bodies of the targeted business typically is insufficient to have a lasting effect on the longer-term development of that business.

5.1.2.5 Conclusion

Family business owners, buyout managers and external consultants expect private equity investment companies to score well in the categories (1) trust and social compatibility, (2) reputation, expertise and regional connectivity as well as to follow a customized investment approach fitting the needs of the targeted business (3). The certitude of an overly active involvement of the investor ex post, in particular in matters of day-to-day business operations, is viewed to be inhibitory to transaction success (4).

In contrast to the highly rational selection criteria employed on the side of institutional private equity investors when screening potential investment targets, the typical family business owner acts less rational when selecting among private equity investment companies in consideration of a private equity backed succession buyout. This explains why to the family business owner "fit of chemistry" appears to be the most decisive factor when opting for or against a particular investor. Not less important is this factor to buyout managers since a private equity sponsored buyout implies a longer-term collaboration between buyout managers and the private equity investment company ex post.

The private equity investment company's reputation conditions its ability to source investment opportunities and in turn is determined by its level of expertise in closing and realizing investment opportunities. A strong regional connectivity was found to be looked at favourable by family business owners considering a private equity backed succession solution. With regard to investment approach, private equity investment companies are expected to "understand" the businesses they invest in, have the ability to add value and have a long rather than short investment horizon.

Compared to early stage (i.e. venture capital) investments, later stage (i.e. buyout) investments typically are marked by little or no operational involvement of the private equity investment company and foremost circle around the provision of financial resources. In fact, it can be noticed that stage of investment and investment size are inversely related to the level of the private equity investment company's operational involvement.

5.1.3 Expectations towards buyout managers

Statements of interviewees consistently indicate that a qualified management team is the single most relevant precondition in realizing a private equity backed succession buyout. Due to the formative role of the typical family business owner, buyout managers are faced with the challenge to fill the management- and leadership void created when the incumbent owner has left the business. Not only the realization and closure of the transaction itself but in particular the longer-term welfare of the business subject to the buyout is fundamentally dependent on buyout managers. The following chapters analyze and discuss expectations of family business owners, institutional private equity investors and consultants towards buyout managers that were identified to be critical to transaction success.

5.1.3.1 Formal qualifications, experience and risk affinity

The quality of a management decisively conditions a business's value. If this self-evident notion is accepted, the systematic measurement of this dimension assumes a high relevance in context of entrepreneurial actions and in particular of institutional private equity investments. This reasoning is shared equally by family business owners and institutional private equity investors as the following statements highlight:

"When equity is invested in any business sufficient management capacity towards the inside and the outside must be assured." (Family business owner)

"A good management can make a bad business flourish while a good business with bad management will most certainly perish ..." (Institutional private equity investor)

A private equity backed succession buyout implies a radical change in the ownership structure of the targeted business. Connected therewith oftentimes are new respectively more stringent entrepreneurial directions, detailed expectations with regard to capital- and turnover efficiency, a refocusing of product- and service offerings respectively efficiency enhancement of production processes and -structures. This confronts buyout managers with new challenges. According to interviewed family business owners and institutional private equity investors the decisive question to ask is whether buyout managers not only from a functional/technical but also from an emotional/personal perspective are able and willing to face these challenges. The most frequently mentioned criteria of interview partners for the evaluation of buyout managers can be grouped into *formal qualifications*, *experience* and *risk-affinity*.

Formal qualifications: Although no interviewee gave explicit descriptions with regard to formal qualifications of buyout managers, most interviewees underscored that minimum standards with regard to formal qualifications of buyout managers exist. As part of a due diligence led by an institutional private equity investor a management audit typically screens for the following competency specifications (Spies/Thess 2005: 164):

- *Leadership*: Value-oriented management, peak performance, inside stability, independence and emotional balance, conflict resolution and communicative abilities.
- *Value adding*: Anticipation- and control of risks, alignment of business policy with value drivers, assumption of responsibility for achievement of objectives and operating profit.
- *Customer- and market orientation*: Negotiation and persuasion skills, social competence, active definition and consequent realization of customer requests and inducement of customer requests and customer demands.
- *Entrepreneurial skill*: Strategic thinking and acting, development and realization of innovative ideas, active change management.
- *Intercultural expertise*: Knowledge of international markets, work experience therein, liaison with different social and cultural environments.
- *Process know-how*: Holistic thinking and acting in the execution of processes, incorporation of interests of individual business segments/units and the larger organization, cultivation of comprehensive thinking and acting, establishment and deployment of synergies.
- *Integration skills*: Ability to build networks, to cope with antagonism and uncertainties, ability to align different interests and elaborate tradeoffs.
- *Functional expertise*: Task- and position relevant knowledge and experience, might include work experience, academic education and functional competencies.

This rather generic catalogue of competencies highlights that the formal assessment of a buyout manager does not differ substantially from the assessment of management potential for conventional management assignments. It also becomes clear that the sufficient specification of itemized criteria is implicated by a multitude of other factors, in particular experience and risk affinity discussed next.

Experience: Interviewees from the group of institutional private equity investors mentioned that *industry specific experience* of managers is a key requirement when considering the financial backing of buyout managers. This corresponds to previous research identifying a "fundamental understanding" of the targeted business's industry sector and previous "successful activities" within that sector to be desirable attributes of buyout managers (Luippold 1991. 61). Other research further indicates that in particular prior *experience in management functions* significantly influences investment return and risk of insolvency in businesses subject to buyout transactions (Schefczyk 2000: 143).

However, symptomatic in the context of family businesses oftentimes is the non-existence or the lack of a sufficiently experienced second management layer (cp. also chapter 5.1.1.4). Family business owners on their part often mention the lack of qualification of line managers and employees as a principle reason why they do not delegate leadership responsibility (Grochla et al. 1984: 407). However, the reasons for family business owner's reluctance to delegate managerial responsibility must be put in perspective. For example, family business owners surveyed by Grochla et al. ranked "adequate education" fifth as meaningful for the delegation of managerial responsibility after other personality traits of managers such as "sense of responsibility" and "reliability" (Grochla et al. 1984: 408). This points to the dependency of the extent of delegation on the owner's appraisal of both the professional and personal aptitude of individual managers.

At the same time, other empirical studies indicate that family businesses offer their line managers much less opportunity to attend regular professional training than non-family businesses (Freund 2000: 187).[13] Reasons commonly put forward for the lack of professional training programs are financial expenditures associated with the development and execution of such programs and the need to find suitable replacements for employees during training sessions. Nevertheless, more than half (55 percent) of family businesses surveyed by Freund indicated their intention to intensify their efforts to organize qualification measures in the future (Freund 2000: 187). This intention indicates that the qualification of line managers and employees in family businesses - also in preparation of succession - is increasingly recognized.

Risk affinity: With regard to *risk affinity*, buyout managers necessarily need to be willing to assume full stewardship of the targeted business and be able to accept risks associated with self-employment.

"It makes a considerable difference if a manager is investing third parties' monies or if he is not only investing his own money but is also liable for business ventures that fail." (Consultant)

13 Two-thirds of family businesses surveyed train their line managers in the areas of communication and presentation skills. Seminars focused on self-management assume the second most important value, followed by problem-solving skills in conflict situations (Freund 2000: 187).

The critical role of risk affinity and the ability of buyout managers to assume risk was confirmed in several statements of interviewees, for example:

"The conversion of a corporate mentality to the entrepreneurial mentality is a major source of difficulty and the biggest trauma the buyout team will face." (Institutional private equity investor)

Interviewed private equity investors stated that a close analysis of each manager's capacity to perform the transition from a salaried to a self-dependent, entrepreneurial position is essential prior to all MBO/MBI transactions. Luippold in this context refers to the necessity of a sufficient existence of "entrepreneurial initiative" (Luippold 1990: 61). In particular since buyout managers most likely used to be salaried employees during all of their professional life and, via the buyout, for the first time gain entrepreneurial independence and -responsibility. Hence, also Luippold stresses the importance of the assessment of such issues (cp. Luippold 1990: 61).

Since for the MBO/MBI per definition only one (principal) round of financing by the private equity investment company is earmarked, pressure on buyout managers to perform well is accordingly high. Buyout managers are challenged to realize the targeted business's potential as presented in the business plan and in line with agreed on milestones defined by the private equity investment company and other financial sponsors (cp. Nathusius/Böhm 2003: 435). Imminent sanctions by both equity- and debt investors if performance lacks behind agreed on targets puts considerable additional pressure on buyout managers.

5.1.3.2 Team composition and team stability

Situations exist in which the fundamental parameters of entrepreneurial demand change, e.g. in cases of strategic repositioning. That might implicate that the incumbent management talent and -potential aligned to the "old" strategy is not able to satisfy demands of the "new", amended strategy. As interviewees from the group of institutional private equity investors mentioned, such situations often occur in context of changes in the business's ownership structure, as is the case in succession incidences. Demands with regard to the management's competencies then often change due to a change in strategy. If a new strategy is not fully implementable with incumbent management structures, changes to that structure are inevitable. Similarly Kell argues that the potential of a management team is never absolutely ascertainable but contingent on the demands of the business strategy followed (cp. Kell 2005: 150).

As interviewed private equity investors indicated, the question on whether an incumbent management team or an external management team is better suited to realize a private equity backed succession scenario must be answered case by case and is significantly influenced by the experience and strategy of the private equity investment company. Further, the choice for a MBO or MBI is influenced by factors such as the quality of the incumbent management team, size of the business, its organizational breadth and the general economic condition. Although in Germany succession MBIs appear to be more frequent than succession MBOs (cp. chapter 2.2.1.2), interviewees from different groups indicated that debt providers typically favour MBOs over MBIs. Since buyout managers are assumed to possess intimate knowledge of the targeted business's constitution banks typically rate a management team's buyout as a mark of confidence of the stability and the prospects of the targeted business. Further, with MBOs banks are not concerned about an exhaustive break in leadership continuity. In conclusion, rightly or wrongly debt providers generally associate less risk with MBOs relative to MBIs.

Due to the incumbent management team's intimate knowledge of the targeted business it appears reasonable to assume that institutional private equity investors equally prefer MBOs over MBIs – as long as the incumbent management is sufficiently qualified to take part in the buyout. However, since family business owners oftentimes exclusively assume managerial and leadership responsibility situations in which the transfer of such responsibility to a second-line management was prevented are very common. In addition, private enterprises, in comparison to public enterprises, often have difficulties attracting talented employees in the first place since privately owned enterprises are generally not able to offer prospective employees the same terms of employment as public enterprises. Promotional opportunities are slim, typically because significant management decisions are "chosen on the basis of wealth and willingness to bear risk as well as for decision skills" (Fama/Jensen 1983: 332). Such positions in private firms tend to be held by (family) shareholders. In terms of remuneration, privately owned businesses typically are not willing to offer stock options to their employees due to limited liquidity and the fact that majority shareholders are generally not willing to dilute their control (cp. Lew/Kolodzeij 1993, Morck 1996). Due to these circumstances the entrepreneurial prowess of incumbent managers in family businesses often is not warranted.

For that reason the supplement of external managers or management teams in buyout transactions can be of critical importance (cp. Schwalbach/Brenner 2001: 166 et sqq.). In context of a prospective MBO this procedure can be of particular relevance if the incumbent management team possesses comprehensive technical- and/or product expertise but is lacking leadership skills. As interviewees from the group of institutional private equity investors pointed out, a practical solution in such cases is a buyin management buyout (BIMBO), i.e. a takeover of the targeted business with both incumbent and external managers.

"And it is appreciated if a manager says, this and this area I don't feel comfortable on my own and I need this and this support. From these kinds of statements you also get a feel for whether or not a manager is BIMBO capable." (Institutional private equity investor)

If a shortage with regard to entrepreneurial prowess and/or managerial ability of incumbent managers is existent, the private equity investment company seeks to substitute all or some of incumbent managers with more suitable external candidates.

Surprisingly, the majority of interviewed family business owners appeared similarly pragmatic in context of opting for a private equity backed succession scenario involving incumbent or external managers.

"Emotions must not influence decision-making when searching for the best successor (team)." (Family business owner)

Interviewed consultants generally highlighted the importance of complementary qualifications of individual buyout managers. Ideally, the team exhibits all functions relevant to the success of the business. However, adventitious buyin managers are typically confronted with a number of challenges, sometimes more, sometimes less pronounced (Prätsch 2007: 94): (1) Lack of product- and market knowledge, (2) unawareness of in-company structures and processes, (3) abandonment of an assumed good position in a different business, (4) adjustment problems, (5) incumbent employee's lack of willingness to cooperate with new management, (6) lack of insider information on the actual status of the targeted business and (7) invalid assessment of the targeted business's potential yield. Overall, it can be concluded that a successful team of buyout managers exhibits a reciprocal complementation of skills and character traits specific to the management task at hand.

A different aspect of team composition is team size. However, *team size* by itself was not found to be a critical factor to transaction success. The head count of the buyout management team obviously is contingent on the size of the targeted business and the management task at hand. Although a larger management team is better able to compensate the loss of a single individual and live up to the professional demands of business administration, coordination problems and therewith complexity of negotiations are likely to increase concurrently (Luippold 1991: 62). While Hoffmann/Ramke suggest two to six managers depending on the size of the transaction (Hoffmann/Ramke 1990: 43), Lütjen recommends to limit team size to up to four managers since otherwise coordination and reconcilement problems must be anticipated (Lütjen 1992: 54). Interviewees from the group of institutional private equity investors mentioned that the optimal buyout management team comprises two to four managers in most incidences.

In order to achieve transaction success in private equity backed succession buyouts the management team is further expected to appear sufficiently stable. Pronounced *stability* of the management team implies the team's ability to assume management and leadership responsibility in the targeted business over a prolonged period of time. The prominence of this circumstance is exemplified in the fact that in approximately half of all MBO transactions management changes occur within the first two years (cp. Hoffmann/Ramke 1990: 44). For that reason Schiller finds that a precondition for the successful realization of a MBO/MBI is sufficient capacity for teamwork among managers (Schiller 1995: 136).

According to statements of institutional private equity investors conducive to team stability principally is *joint work experience* of team members. A track record of joint work experience receives particular value in cases of a MBI involving managers with no or limited mutual work experience or in cases of a BIMBO involving managers with no mutual work experience.

It became clear from interviewees' statements that a buyout ex post causes managers to accept considerable charges and restrictions over a prolonged period of time. The stability of the buyout team therefore further is impacted by the personal periphery of each manager such as each manager's familial-, financial- and sanitary situation.

"The ideal manager in my view is married and has children." (Institutional private equity investor)

To Luippold, the "microsocial environment" of each involved buyout manager should be subject to detailed review and comprises predominantly of the previous occupational- as well as familial context of each manager (Luippold 1991: 61).

Lastly, stability of a buyout management team is also affected by its relationship to the departing family business owner and the institutional private equity investor. In particular, in case of a MBO the relationship between buyout managers and the departing owner is a sensitive issue, as was stressed by interviewees from the group of consultants. Prospective buyout managers ex ante are principally obligated towards the departing family business owner; however, during the buyout process employed managers migrate into a new role of soon-to-be (co)owners of the targeted business. For that reason a conflict of interests is pre-programmed. Specifically, the retiring owner expects the management to be committed to his/her objective to achieve a high sales price while at the same time the management's objective is to acquire the business at a preferably low price. In this context the conflict potential between the departing family business owner and buyout managers is considerable. Accordingly, destabilization potential within the MBO team increases.

5.1.3.3 Balanced motives and sufficient motivation

In consideration of motives of buyout managers to take part in a buyout, i.e. motives that give the impulse for changing from a salaried to a self-employed position, principally *immaterial* and *material* motives must be differentiated. Interviewees from all groups made statements that indicate that they expect a balanced distribution of these motives among buyout managers.

Interviewed buyout managers highlighted that among the most prominent *immaterial (not quantifiable) motives* for a buyout are the urge for self-actualization, decision-making authority and personal responsibility. Further, Luippold finds that buyout managers might perceive a MBO/MBI as a resort out of a "career holdup" in conjunction with a gain in status and prestige which is typically associated with a change from a salaried position to self-employment (cp. Luippold 1991: 42). Often, a buyout also is associated with the urge to avoid risks connected to the establishment of a new business venture. In particular in the case of a MBO, business risk for buyout managers is readily assessable since the management team possesses insider knowledge of the targeted business's constitution (cp. Ballwieser/Schmid 1990: 303). In the case of a MBI, business risk for the management team presumably is greater but might be mitigated by a high level of industry knowledge and professionalism (cp. chapter 5.1.3.1).

The *material (quantifiable) motives* for managers to transact a buyout foremost are manifested in the opportunity to achieve above average monetary success. In context of a self-dependent buyout the strongest material motive is the chance to acquire a relatively large equity share in the targeted business (respectively the targeted business's management company). In addition to earning a fixed salary, the equity stake enables buyout managers to receive dividend distributions and realize proceeds when divesting their shareholding at a later point in time. In order to come to a sales agreement, buyout managers necessarily must allocate a higher value to the targeted business respectively the targeted business's equity stake than the departing owner (Luippold 1991. 42).

Interviewees from the group of institutional private equity investors indicated that buyout managers generally aim to limit the financial exposure in the businesses they invest in, e.g. to diversify their personal portfolio. This circumstance leads to the discussion of a buyout manager's adequate *motivation.* In the context of a private equity backed buyout financial sponsors typically ask buyout managers to get involved strongly financially in the targeted business. According to the concept of "bonding" in line with agency theory, financial sponsors hope to elevate the buyout managers' motivation and commitment towards the targeted business. Similar observations are also found in the literature (cp. Schefczyk 2006: 200).

"Principally I want a manager that invests good and sensible money according to the size of the transaction and personal ability. However the size of the investment should never ruin the existence of the manager. If managers are uncertain about how to pay the rent, their decision-making will be intimidated. That can not be right, however losses must hurt him markedly." (Institutional private equity investor)

Per definition the buyout management team's acquisition of a significant equity stake in the target business is the distinctive characteristic of every buyout and, for that reason, must be regarded as a critical success factor in succession buyouts involving institutional private equity investors. Several times interviewees pointed out that critical to transaction success is the ability to appropriately motivate buyout managers ex post and to align interests of the private equity investor with those of the buyout managers. In his study Jakoby confirmed that the extent of the equity participation determines the motivation of the management team and the long-term success of the MBO/MBI transaction (Jakoby 2000: 427). In principle these results correspond with the predications of agency theory which essentially argues that a meaningful financial participation of a management team in the affected business diminishes agency conflicts while having positive effects on the development of the business (cp. Jensen/Meckling 1976). The extent of the equity participation of the management team should be chosen in that way that the individual shareholding stands in an adequate proportion to the overall wealth of the individual manager.[14] As one interviewee expressed:

"Managers should have enough 'skin in the game' to care about their company, but not so much that they might be overly conservative. The downside has to

14 Cp. similar results by Shleifer/Vishny 1997: 748 et sqq., Backes-Gellner et al. 2002: 63 et sqq., Hammer/Bräuch 2002: 82.

hurt, but not too much. The upside has to be sweet." (Institutional private equity investor)

Different interviewees indicated that the financing structure of the business subject to the buyout should award the management team with a preferably large equity stake in the business. One interviewee from the group of consultants mentioned that a sufficient incentive system entails an equity participation of managers of at least one to three times their annual remuneration. The participation of the complete management team in the equity of the targeted business should be at least five percent. Further, contracts between buyout managers and private equity investment companies should make use of agreements to elevate the buyout management team's equity holding under specific premises. If, for example, predefined targets (e.g. sales revenues) are exceeded, the buyout management team should be able to increase its share in the business's nominal capital by a fixed percentage. These so-called "step-ups" represent an additive financial incentive for additional performance (cp. Hoffmann/Ramke 1990: 69, Luippold 1991: 62).

Interview partners also mentioned *initiative* and the existence of *alternative employment options* to be indicative of a high level of motivation among buyout managers. Private equity backed succession buyouts might be initiated by the existing family business owner, the private equity investment company or buyout managers. Although interviewees in this study did not specifically mention initiative of buyout managers in context of factors critical to transaction success, interviewees nonetheless underscored the criticality of sustained motivation of buyout managers and their entrepreneurial involvement in targeted businesses ex post. The level of initiative exhibited by buyout managers in the transaction process then is indicative of the level of the team's motivation. This idea corresponds to findings of Kitching who found that for European buyout transactions buyout processes ex post run less successful if they are conducted under the initiative of the vendor (Kitching 1989). Similarly, Hanney (1986) found that in more than 50 percent of successful MBOs in the UK the initiative for the buyout emanated from the buyout management team. Finally, interviewees indicated that alternative employment options for buyout managers prior to the MBO/MBI are indicative of a high level of motivation of these managers and that these - ceteris paribus - increase the potential for transaction success.

5.1.3.4 Long-term involvement and vision for the business

Family business owners and private equity investment companies expect buyout managers to convincingly signal their intention to stay involved long-term in the targeted business and to have a clear *vision* for the future of the business subject to the buyout.

The business policy of private equity investment companies a priori envisions equity participations in portfolio companies over a limited period of time. The duration of the participation can vary considerably but typically ranges between three to eight years and usually does not outlive a 10 year tenure at the longest. The central criterion for the qualification of a buyout is that buyout managers - next to pursuing financial interests - primarily seek to realize their entrepreneurial ambitions. To that extent, a partial sale of the buyout management team's equity stake at some point in time principally is not harmful to the qualification of a transaction as a MBO/MBI; however, an exhaustive disposal of the buyout management team's equity stake within a time frame similar to the investment horizon of a private equity investment company would be harmful to such qualification (cp. Luippold 1991: 70 et sqq.).

A convenient exit route for the private equity investment company is the divestment of the equity stake in the targeted business to buyout managers. The attractive aspect of this internal solution is that in context of a change to the shareholder structure no new investors add to the existing. Buyout managers therefore might be granted pre-emption rights or predefined purchase options. The latter alternative has the advantage to the buyout manager that the purchase price can be fixed ex ante and is not contingent on offers of third parties. Through this a basic objective of the buyout is achieved, since buyout managers are destined to become fully independent business owners. However, an equity acquisition by the buyout management team at last always depends on the financial strength of individual members of the team (cp. Luippold 1991: 70). It can be expected that the buyout management team's credible intention to acquire all or the majority of ownership rights in the targeted business ex post contributes positively to the likelihood of transaction success. To the family business owner and the private equity investment company this intention signals the long-term orientation of buyout managers paired with a high level of commitment and motivation.

Both the family business owner's and the institutional private equity investor's assessment of the quality of buyout managers - including the credibility of their commitment to stay involved long-term - is contingent on the buyout manager's business plan. Prior to any serious consideration of backing a particular buyout management team, institutional private equity investors expect to receive a detailed business plan specifying information relevant for characterization of the business's purpose, initial valuation and development potential. The business plan substantiates a business venture and highlights how management intends to realize the business's potential. The creation and configuration of such a plan insofar is the first probation test for buyout managers since authors are urged to demonstrate their ability to present measures lifting the targeted business's potential. Although a buyout management team seeking financing is tempted to present itself in a preferably positive light, the private equity investment company's assessment of the quality of the business plan is contingent on the factuality and plausibility of its data. Necessarily, the description of risks and problems potentially impacting on the business's success as well as the delineation of methods of resolution of such issues make elementary constituents of a convincing business plan. The concealment of self-evident risks, on the other hand, generally has disadvantageous effects (cp. Mayer 2003: 135).

When reviewing a business plan, a private equity investment company primarily is interested in good and relevant arguments that promise business growth. According to Schwetje/Vaseghi a convincing business plan has three essential features. The first feature is a detailed depiction of short- and long-term objectives; the second feature is a careful description of how the objectives can be achieved in realistic general conditions; the third feature circles around a description of how the realization of the plan will meet the expectations of equity investors (Schwetje/Vaseghi 2007: 1). With regard to structure, convincing business plans are geared towards those areas of business management that are critical for the success of the business venture. Typically these can be split in the following eight components (cp. Pichotta 1990: 56 et sqq.): (1) Overview of the business's purpose; (2) illustration of the (corporate) organization; (3) specification of the product(s) and service(s) respectively; (4) analysis of the associated industry sector and the relevant market(s); (5) arrangement of marketing and sales activities; (6) presentation of management; (7) budgeted operating statement and balance sheet for upcoming 3-5 years; (8) evaluation and assertion of capital needs.

Interviewed private equity investors emphasized that they essentially seek to know how and in which period of time a return on investment is realizable when screening a business plan. Investors typically first pay attention to how the business's past achievements are described, the unique selling proposition of products and/or services, the feasibility of outlined measures to achieve the business's objectives as well as the quality and experience of the management team. Not least, the quality of the business plan itself is perceived to be one indicator of the buyout management team's quality and its ability to envision a promising future for the targeted business.

5.1.3.5 Conclusion

Buyout managers assume the most central role in the success of a private equity backed succession buyout ex post. Although the intrinsic qualities of buyout managers will only be revealed ex post, the notional qualities of buyout managers substantially impact on the course of the transaction process and the achievability of transaction success.

The analysis of interviews found that interviewees from the groups of family business owners, institutional private equity investors and consultants consider formal qualifications, experience and risk affinity (1) coupled with a sustainable, high level of motivation (2) to be the most critical attributes of buyout managers. In addition, also the composition and presumable stability of the management team (3) in connection with a credible demonstration of the intention to stay involved long-term in the targeted business (4) are critical to successfully realize a private equity backed succession buyout.

Both institutional private equity investors and family business owners expect to find indicators that make buyout managers appear sufficiently committed to the targeted business's welfare and perpetuation. Next to an emotional commitment this claim imperatively comprises a financial commitment in form of an equity participation meaningful in context of each buyout manager's personal financial situation. Ideally, buyout managers should be locked-in twofold: with their reputation and with personal wealth.

5.1.4 Involvement of consultants and other financial intermediaries

Next to the participants in the private equity backed succession buyout process discussed so far typically a number of other parties get involved that contribute to individual phases of the transaction process. Interviewed family business owners, institutional private equity investors and buyout managers indicated that the involvement of parties specified in this chapter is critical to the success of private equity backed succession buyouts.

5.1.4.1 Consultants

Since private equity investment companies are relatively small business organizations with a slim personnel structure they principally rely on external professional support pre- and post execution of an investment. Similarly, family businesses typically do not employ in-house resources specialized on the structuring of business divestures. For that reason they are equally dependent on acquiring expertise from external sources. At the same time, buyout managers are in need of professional consulting support since they usually do not have relevant experience in the execution of a buyout. At last, the speed at which a buyout must be realized, e.g. due to the presumed existence of lucrative counter offers, is an argument in favour of involving experienced consultants in the process. With increasing complexity, i.e. in particular with increasing size of the transaction, generally also the number of consultants involved in the execution of the transaction increases. According to the majority of interviewees an early involvement of qualified consultants is advisable and spares mislead investments in time and cost.

Integral for success of a private equity backed succession buyout is the design of a customized company law- and tax concept meeting the financing- and succession needs of each individual case.[15] Interview partners from all groups confirmed that *legal- and tax counsels* are indispensable to transaction success of any buyout. Assignments range from legal counselling in first negotiations between contract partners to contributions in the legal acquisition structuring - in particular in cases of international transactions involving different jurisdictions - to the composition of detailed and often extremely complex agreements and contracts. In this context it appears critical that legal counsels also understand the economic context underlying each transaction. This aspect is of particular importance since in-house legal counsels often mandated on the side of family businesses are unlikely to be specifically trained in legal matters relevant to corporate finance.

"Family businesses often mandate their family lawyer or tax consultant with advisory ..." (Consultant)

If this is the case, vendors should engage more specialized legal counsels to facilitate negotiations "at eye level" with the acquirer's team of counsels, as different statements of interviewees indicate.

"... I often see processes fail due to poor consulting [on the side of the family business owner]. The use of experts re contract design and tax treatment is very important ..." (Institutional private equity investor)

Especially a highly leveraged business can much less afford to be inefficiently structured from a tax perspective than businesses with a relative high equity ratio. The tax specific optimization therefore assumes major relevance within the legal structuring of the buyout. This substantially contributes to the targeted

15 For some specific legal- and tax issues compare chapter 5.2.2.

business's ability to generate the required cashflows ex post and thus to the realization of the transaction itself. For that reason, tax counsels commissioned to structure the tax-based part of the overall transaction concept contribute fundamentally to the success or failure of the transaction.[16]

An indispensable function of *auditors* is to generate appraisal reports as the basis for the determination of sales/purchase prices of targeted businesses. In addition, interviewed institutional private equity investors mentioned that auditors might be commissioned with the analysis of specific problem areas, e.g. a retroactive consolidation of individual financial statements, analyses of respectively plausibility tests for financial forecasts or the assignment of book values to balance sheet positions such as inventory or receivables. Occasionally, services of consultants discussed above (commercial lawyer, commercial tax consultant and auditor) are integrated in one consultancy firm offering integrated consulting with potentially considerable synergistic effects for clients.

According to interviewees from the group of consultants *investment banks and M&A consultants* appear to assume an increasing relevance. This holds true in particular for transactions with a transaction value in excess of EUR 50 million. Here, investment banks and M&A consultants assume similar functions. These are twofold: On one hand investment banks and M&A consultants provide dealflow for the private equity investment company while on the other hand these parties are able to establish competition, i.e. at least signal potential acquirers that competition prevails. In short, investment banks and M&A consultants deliver market-like conditions. However, "competition" not necessarily connotes an auction or a controlled sales process. Often it is sufficient if the potential acquirer believes or fears that additional interested acquirers are existent. However, two interviewees indicated that the involvement of an investment bank or M&A consultant might be disadvantageous in certain cases. The reason is that M&A consultants and investment banks have a strong interest in achieving a high sales price in the divestment process. For that reason they are likely to search for additional sales options respectively make vendors aware of the spectrum of divestment routes and the level of sales prices possibly realizable. This potentially protracts the divestment process. Investment banks and M&A consultants often also constitute difficult negotiation partners in the eyes of potential acquirers and for that reason might cause potential acquirers to not submit an

16 It is not possible to address the complex legal- and tax specific aspects of a private equity backed succession buyout in more detail in this study. Comprehensive literature pertaining to legal- and taxation issues in context of business succession already exists (cp. chapter 1.3).

offer for anticipation of high prices and a prolonged divestment process (cp. Holzapfel/Pöllath 2000: 10). The involvement of an investment bank or M&A consultant thus might counteract with the vendor's objectives to close the transaction quickly ("transaction speed") and to engage in processes that have a high probability of success ("certainty of transaction closure").

Other functions generally associated with the involvement of investment banks respectively M&A consultants are control and discipline of the buyout process. In addition, the services of such consultants typically comprise the execution or support of the following: Compilation of sales documents ("book"); selection of potentially interested acquirers ("long- and short list"); completion of non-disclosure agreements; selective issuance of information, control of flow of information ("data room"); selection of interested parties for final negotiations; final negotiations and contract closure (cp. Holzapfel/Pöllath 2000: 10 et sq.). These functions, however, might also be deliverable by others, in particular by professional vendors themselves or other advisors including legal counsels or auditors. Since an unorganized respectively insufficiently professional divestment process constitutes a considerable risk to transaction success, vendors typically carefully balance costs and benefits associated with the involvement of investment banks or M&A consultants.

Alongside the consulting services of the groups mentioned up to now a comprehensive and differentiated market for freelance consulting services for departing family business owners and their successors has emerged over the last decade (Schröer/Kayser 2006: 2 et sq). Next to process steering services, integrated succession counselling assumes a great relevance among the rendered services. In this context, interviewed consultants see great demand for *mediators* that balance the interests of transferors and transferees.

"In order to fully live up to expectations of the client, consultants must appreciate both sides (i.e. the vendor's and the acquirer's side) of the transaction." (Consultant)

Considering the conflict potential due to the principal differences in the mind set of family business owners and institutional private equity investors in addition to the opportunity costs of process abandonment, the involvement of consultants focusing on mediation between the principally involved parties in private equity backed succession buyouts can assume critical relevance in certain situations.

Case by case the private equity investment company might involve other *specialized consultants* in the realization of the buyout transaction, in particular during the due diligence phase. According to interviewees' statements these consultants support the private equity investment company in business plan screening and business valuation (corporate finance consultants), in conducting management audits in order to assess the qualifications of individual managers or selected parts of the workforce (HR consultants) or in supporting commercial due diligence activities (strategy consultants) for procurement of market information and identification of specific market risks.

Overall, it appears that not only the choice of the "right" consultant, but the *fit of chemistry* among effectively acting individuals is critical to transaction success. As became clear from conducted interviews, a promising procedure in selecting consultants is to look for routine and reputation in context of the desired course of action (e.g. "rigidity" vs. "flexibility"). Most important, however, appears to be complementation and fit of chemistry among those acting on one side.

Lastly, although the majority of private equity backed succession buyout processes seem to be initiated by departing family business owners, most *initial contacts* between the family business owner and the private equity investment company appear to be established through consultants which underscores the paramount role of these service providers in the transaction process. Even though few buyout cases might be initiated by consultants, consultants nevertheless assume an important role in establishing and nurturing contacts between family business owners, institutional private equity investors and buyout managers. Due to this circumstance one interviewed consultant likened his role in private equity succession buyouts to that of a "bridge builder":

"The role of consultants at the very start of the process often resembles that of bridge builders." (Consultant)

Due to diverse statements of interviewees the author was unable to rank intermediaries according to their ability or likelihood to establish contacts between family businesses and private equity investment companies. However, it appears that at least for larger transactions such contacts are most often established by dedicated M&A consultants or investment banks. Next to other consultants discussed above, interview partners pointed out that industry associations and lobby groups are likely to assume an increasingly active role in facilitating contacts between family business owners, private equity investment companies and buyout managers.

5.1.4.2 Other financial intermediaries

Since equity capital resources of buyout managers typically are insufficient for the acquisition of a medium-sized family business, additional capital resources for the realization of the transaction are needed. Next to private equity investment companies, the operability of a buyout typically involves other parties that provide essential financing functions. These are institutions that procure senior- and subordinated debt as well as mezzanine capital.

As the primary providers of debt obviously great relevance is attached to commercial banks. Depending on business policy and the degree of involvement in the buyout process these institutions might also provide comprehensive consulting services (Luippold 1991: 47). Since a MBO/MBI transaction requires financial resources that often by far outreach the rules of conventional lending, banks seek to conduct extensive analyses of the targeted business and its acquirers as well as to create customized and flexible financing solutions. Commercial banks in principle prefer the placing of senior debt collateralized by non-current assets and/or current assets. Since assets of the targeted business oftentimes constitute insufficient collateral for the required level of debt borrowing, banks must be ready to project the targeted business's future cashflows and accept these as collateral for their engagement. Out of risk considerations merchant banks typically build a syndicate prior to the financing of a takeover or syndicate loans to other banks after issued credit assurance. Depending on the scope of the financial engagement banks assume a more or less pronounced agency function for their capital providers (Luippold 1991: 48 et sq.).

According to interviewed institutional private equity investors the merchant bank's main contribution to the buyout process is the structuring of an optimal financing structure. Due to buyout manager's limited experience and expertise in executing a buyout, a situational, customized service is critical to transaction success. Consulting services are not limited to the preparation and execution of the buyout process. Debt providers intensively monitor the development of the buyout business and make use of their codetermination rights in case of misdirected developments. In this context an entrepreneurial, truly partnership-like collaboration between debt- and equity investors is of utmost importance. In summary, the existence of a sufficiently large number of debt providers and the quality of the relationship with them constitute critical success factors in typical cases of private equity backed succession buyouts.

Providers of subordinated debt typically are other private equity investment companies or dedicated mezzanine funds. Mezzanine funds participate in buyout transactions with subordinated debt and/or equity-like instruments, e.g. in form of conversion- or option rights. Case-by-case also traditional debt providers might provide mezzanine capital to supplement the financing structure of buyout transactions. In that way, some merchant banks and less risk-averse insurance companies might provide subordinated loans, in few cases even in combination with equity-like instruments (De Ridder 1990: 50 et sqq).

5.1.4.3 Conclusion

Interviewees from all reference groups stressed the important role of professional consultants during different phases of the buyout transaction process.

Private equity investment companies categorically rely on legal-/tax advisors and auditors in buyout transactions in order to minimize risk of insufficient business analysis. Further, the elaboration of complex purchase contracts and far-reaching financial- and legal due diligence apparently requires support from appropriate experts. To some extent the involvement of external experts in the due diligence phase also is demanded by debt providers.

Similarly, vendors rely on external legal-/tax advisors and auditors in the divestment process. While the level of trust and emotional bondage to long-term "house advisors" repeatedly mandated for varied assignments is likely to be high, vendors typically are better off integrating larger, on M&A transactions specialized law-/tax- and auditing firms. These firms allow for negotiation "at eye level" with consortia of potential acquirers backed by institutional private equity investors and their teams of experienced, specialized advisors.

Process focused consultants are of help particularly if businesses for sale are small and the vendor and its team of advisors has had little or no relevant experience in steering divestment processes. For larger transaction, such services are offered by dedicated M&A advisors and investment banks. Although M&A advisors and investment banks are unlikely to accelerate transaction processes, they are able to organize market-like conditions ("competition") thereby presumably maximizing sale proceeds.

At last, both transferors and transferees need to be aware that all groups of advisors discussed in this chapter principally act out of self-interest which, if not anticipated and adequately implicated, in some cases might also hinder the transaction process. Therefore, remuneration for consultants ideally should be performance related to a large extent.

Since equity capital resources of buyout managers typically are insufficient for the takeover of a business, capital from external sources is needed. This accentuates the high relevance of financial intermediaries providing equity- and debt instruments to succession buyouts. While in theory it is possible to acquire external capital exclusively in form of debt, the default risk of borrowed capital increases with its share of the total financing volume.

5.2 Framework conditions

The analysis of framework conditions is subdivided in expectations towards the targeted business (chapter 5.2.1) and expectations towards the external environment (5.2.2). While chapter 5.2.1 discusses those expectations of institutional private equity investors, buyout managers and consultants towards the targeted business identified to be critical to realizing a private equity backed succession buyout, chapter 5.2.2 analyzes statements from interviewees pertaining to external environmental conditions.

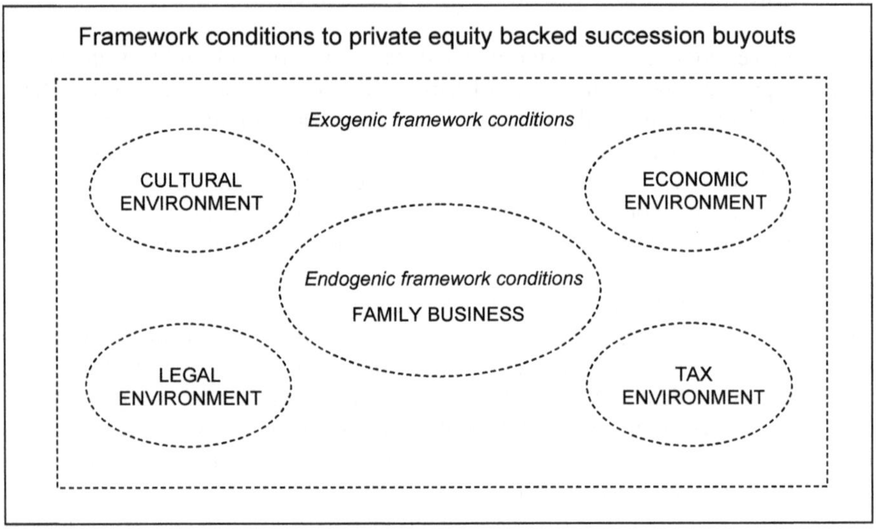

Figure 27: Framework conditions to PE backed succession buyouts.
Source: Author's illustration.

5.2.1 Expectations towards the targeted business

Principal objective of an institutional private equity investor in realizing a buyout is a lasting increase in the targeted business's value. Next to measures of efficiency enhancement this often is achieved in the optimization of the targeted business's risk-/return profile. Ideally a business exhibits a reciprocal relationship between financial- and operative risk (Mittendorfer 2001: 142). For the realization of a buyout in particular those businesses are suitable that exhibit low financial- as well as operative risk. In context of a buyout transaction the financial risk of the targeted business increases by the amount of debt ("leverage") incurred. In order to limit overall risk of the transaction the suitability of a business for the realization of a buyout then must be assessed on grounds of a number of factors that signal low operative risk.

5.2.1.1 Cashflow generation and earning power

Cashflow generation: In a private equity investment company's appraisal of the operability of a buyout the cashflow assumes a dominating relevance. The cashflow signals the aptitude of a business to finance investments and dividend distributions from ordinary operations (self-financing). At the same time the cashflow determines the business's capacity for debt service being of particular relevance in case of buyout transactions. Interviewees from the group of institutional private equity investors stated that businesses with high, stable and predictable cashflows are most suitable for the realization of a MBO/MBI since for these businesses the debt service capacity can be readily determined and the risk of default is reduced.

These findings are congruent with the results of previous studies making use of financial indicators to identify the suitability of MBO/MBI candidate businesses. The growth, stability and rate of cashflow of buyout candidate businesses was researched in these studies and identified to be a central determinant of the operability of a MBO/MBI.[17] Although the assessment methods and the observation periods vary considerably, these previous studies arrive at the concordant proposition, that a high- and stable cashflow is a reliable indicator for a business's potential to develop successfully after a MBO/MBI.

Earning power: Directly related to a business's ability to generate cash is its profitability. Buyout candidate businesses only make attractive investment targets if they are able to fulfil the return expectations of their financial sponsors. To answer the question whether a SME principally makes an attractive investment target for a private equity investment company return on equity of that business can be compared with the investment return demanded by that investor. Private equity investment companies typically expect a return on investment in excess of 20 percent p.a. (IRR). Figure 28 shows returns of SME according to business size. Particularly interesting here are the returns on equity. Depending on business size these lie between 12 and 24 percent although diminishing with increasing turnover. This phenomenon is explainable by low equity quotas in

17 Cp. Singh 1990, Kaplan/Stein 1993, Jakoby 2000

particular of small businesses. For businesses with stable profitability a reduced equity quota necessarily pushes the return on the amount of equity put to work. In addition, it should be noted that the observed profit margins are pre-tax expenditures. If consistent equity ratios and tax expenditures are accounted for return on equity would be lower, in particular for smaller businesses. Further, illustrated figures are median values implying that half of surveyed businesses are more profitable than displayed.

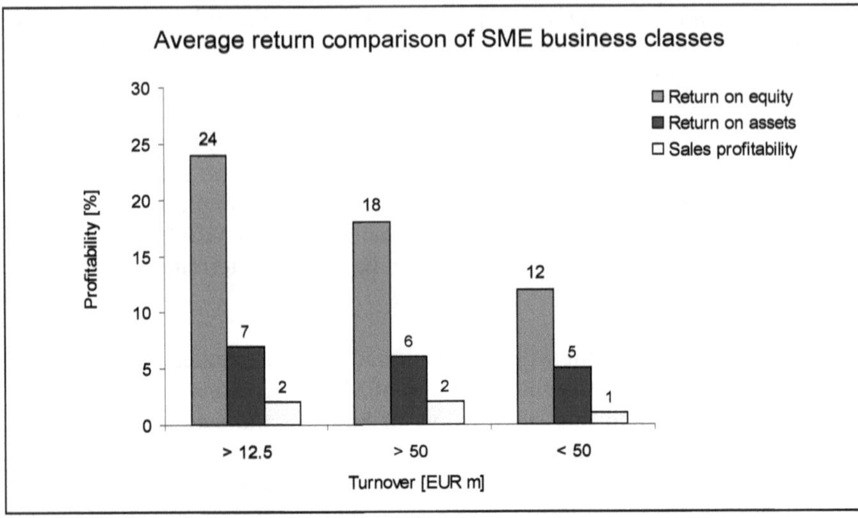

Figure 28: Average return comparison of SME business classes.
Source: Author's illustration based on Deutscher Sparkassen- und Giroverband 2004b: 11/16/41.

Since tax implications remained unaccounted for and inconsistent equity quotas are included in the sample no conclusive statements about the number or sizes of SME that hold up to the return expectations of private equity investment companies is possible. However, it can be assumed that a substantial number of these businesses would be able to fulfill investment return expectations of at least 20 percent p.a. (IRR).

Often in literature also low *capital expenditures* of MBO/MBI candidate businesses is claimed (cp. Leopold et al. 2003: 24) since capital expenditures strain liquidity, i.e. consume cash that can not be used for debt service. However, a low level of capital expenditures was not explicitly mentioned by interviewed institutional private equity investors in this study when asked for expectations towards buyout candidate businesses. Similarly, Forst has argued that "catch-up investments” per se are not an obstacle to the realization of a MBO/MBI since they have to be executed by every sensible investor and thus ultimately should solely depress the purchase price (Forst 1992: 39). At the same time capital expenditures should not be overly high due to an initial high drain of cash caused by servicing debt payments. For that reason a preference for businesses with an endowment of seasonable capital goods can principally be affirmed. Instead, the existence of non-operating assets without any strategic importance and the potential of their disposition are generally accepted to be favourable (Hoffmann/Ramke 1990: 49).

Literature also often mentions a *low debt ratio* as a precondition for realizing a MBO/MBI in a targeted business (cp. Leopold et al. 2003: 24). However, within the scope of this study, the level of net debt was also not found to be a critical factor determining transaction success. The scope of debt financing in form of secured loans is determined by the rate of cashflow and the existent, unused collateral (Mittendorfer 2001: 144). However, the demand for a low level of debt in buyout candidate businesses per se can not be followed since the absence of debt implies a higher purchasing price. Consequently, the aspired effect of a higher debt financing potential principally is neutralized.

5.2.1.2 Market positioning and size

It is obvious that a business's earning power is conditioned by its market positioning. For that reason businesses with an above average competitive position (i.e. market position) are most suitable for the realization of MBO/MBI transactions as interviewed institutional private equity investors affirmed. Similarly, Albach/Freund verified empirically that between the successful completion of generational change as well as the market positioning of the business a close interdependency exists. Businesses less well positioned from a strategic perspective were found to be affected by higher fluctuation and were less well able to prepare for ownership change financially (Albach/Freund 1989: 141/180).

It appears that buyout focused private equity investors further favour to invest in businesses in industry sectors with *high barriers to entry* and *low competition.* For these reasons businesses active in mature markets are especially sought after. However, *slow growth* and *slow technological advancement* allegedly demanded of the targeted business's market by buyout focused investors would unnecessarily limit the scope of investment opportunities according to one interviewee. In context of the targeted business's product range this implies solely that products respectively the product know-how is tested and offers favourable long-term perspectives. Hoffmann/Ramke characterize a secured market position with an "established and competitive product program and a sufficiently diversified product lineup" (Hoffman/Ramke 1990: 47 et sq.).

At the same time, *long product life cycles* reduce the commercial/distribution risk since the necessity for rapid introduction of successor products with uncertain acceptability can be neglected. Long product life cycles are often found in industry sectors with little technical innovations such as metal processing. However, a buyout candidate business might certainly counteract the risk of high market dynamics and short innovation cycles by specialized competencies such as short product development periods (Frommann 1992: 108).

Further literature often mentions the advantages of a *broad customer spread and -diversification* indicative of competitiveness and resistance to cyclicality. Hoffman/Ramke in particular recommend to probe dependency on customers or suppliers when screening a business for buyout suitability (Hoffmann/Ramke 1990: 48).

Closely related to the above mentioned aspects is the targeted business's *size.* A firm, above-average market position generally is constituted on a minimum level of business size, at least a size that allows the business to capitalize on economies of scale. Without discussing the reciprocal relationship of market position and business size in any more detail it is important to notice that a minimum business size is critical to the realization of a private equity backed succession solution for a second reason.

Interviewed institutional private equity investors stated that the majority of family businesses in Germany are simply too small to make attractive investment targets to them. As was discussed in chapter 2.1.2 the group of German family businesses is characterized by a large number of small and medium-sized businesses (enterprise value < EUR 50 million) as well as a relatively small number of large businesses (enterprise value > EUR 50 million). Even private equity investment companies targeting small buyout transactions nowadays target businesses with annual turnover of approximately > EUR 2.5 million intending to invest equity capital of approximately > EUR 0.5 million. Accordingly, institutional private equity (excluding private equity capital from state-run investment programs, business angels or other private sources) is only available to those businesses able to accommodate the minimum investment sizes of these private equity investment companies.

Statements from different interviewees further indicate that investment in small family businesses typically poses the danger that essential reporting-, controlling-, and planning systems are not (sufficiently) existent and monitoring of the investment is difficult or impracticable (cp. chapter 5.2.1.4). On a more general term concerning "size" in context of business acquisitions Pearson finds: "It is preferable that the size of the company to be acquired is sufficient for there to be some senior and middle managers currently employed in addition to the divesting shareholder(s)" (Pearson 1988: 26). In that sense it is plausible to assume that private equity investment companies also avoid small businesses since these businesses are less likely to have realized a transition from an intuitive personal- to a systematic formal leadership structure. However, without an established and self-sufficient personnel structure to work with - in particular concerning middle management - private equity investment companies are missing one of their principle investment rationales (cp. also chapter 5.1.1.4).

Despite the pyramid-like dispersion of potential investment targets in the SME segment it must be assumed that the supply of institutional private equity decreases with diminishing size of investment targets. Ironically, it can be constituted that in particular small family businesses are reliant on professional private equity investors in realizing a MBO/MBI. While large family businesses principally make more attractive investment targets to private equity investment companies, these large businesses appear to be less reliant on MBO/MBI succession solutions. This circumstance generally can be attributed to the enlargement of succession alternatives (e.g. implementation of qualified salaried non-family managers) in combination with an increased financing leeway for large family businesses.

5.2.1.3 Organizational structure and information management

Consequences of the agglomeration of leadership and management responsibility in the person of the family business owner are typically a lack of organizational structure and insufficient information management systems. Some authors have described the management structures prevailing in SME as "adhocracy" (cp. Bergamin 1995: 40.). Characteristic to many SME also is the insufficiency of management information systems. Although large corporates are oftentimes overfed with output from management information systems, this does not hold true for the majority of SME (Bussiek 1996: 90).[18] If organizational structures were built intuitively and guidelines for operational conduct have an improvisa-

18 This type of information can only be a basis for *reactive* management measures; with this information target deflection due to various interference variables is detected. This allows the management to *readjust* the course of action; however, it can not appoint the course itself (cp. Bussiek 1995: 90).

tional character a number of problems arise in context of realizing a private equity backed succession buyout.

"The more professional a business was run in the past, the less work to be done for us." (Institutional private equity investor)

Problems associated with insufficiently pronounced organizational structures and ineffective information management systems appear to affect buyout managers and institutional private equity investors likewise.

In family businesses with owners that omitted establishing independent business units with largely independent line managers, opportunities for incumbent managers to assume leadership responsibility and acquire skills invaluable to realizing a buyout were largely forfeited (cp. chapter 5.1.1.4). In such cases the assignment of external managers and the realization of a MBI might appear to be a feasible succession solution. However, interviewed consultants indicated that also for external successors entry into businesses lacking an adequate organizational structure proves to be particularly difficult in most cases. External (buyin) managers in those situations are facing impeding circumstances in gaining an overview of business events and in finding access to management-relevant information. A non-existence of clearly delineated organizational structures and an inadequacy of information management systems typically prove extremely challenging to buyin managers that have not "grown" with the targeted businesses and that are unable to follow the departing owner's unstructured, intuitive management style. It is immediately evident that if only fragmented information e.g. about the targeted business's productivity exists, misguided developments for buyin managers are difficult to identify and address appropriately.

Similarly Koch/Wegmann argue that one of the principal prerequisites for the implementation of an effective management is the implementation of an effective accounting- and controlling system. Flaws in organizing an effective accounting- and controlling system will also lead to flawed decision-making or late corrections. If cost accounting and calculations are ineffective, management risks investment in loss-generating projects (Koch/Wegmann 2002: 87). These authors argue that principally it is the aspiration of every ambitious management to develop this material into a comprehensive management information (controlling) system that builds the basis for operative actions.

Statements of interviewed institutional private equity investors indicated that the investment proposition of private equity investment companies is based on the ability to accurately track the development of its portfolio businesses. For that reason, prior to executing an investment, private equity investment companies seek to gain sufficient confidence in a targeted business's management information system (in particular accounting-, controlling- and reporting capacities). The non-existence or the insufficient pronouncement of such a system inhibits a private equity investment company's positive investment decision and this constitutes a threat to the realization of a private equity backed succession solution.

Interviewed private equity investors stated that the search for and collection of relevant data in the course of due diligence in businesses with underdeveloped management information systems is tedious and time-intensive. Internal information relating to a business's past financial performance is predominantly issued by a dedicated accounting department. Also information concerning inventory- and performance data as well as other relevant information from business units typically is issued by the accounting department. However, difficult due diligence cases for example are situations in which a business's accounting is completely outsourced to external tax consultants and in which controlling is either non-existent or underdeveloped. The collection of relevant data (e.g. audited financial statements of last three years and budgeted financial statements for next three years) when conducting due diligence on SME can be extremely tedious (Koch/Wegmann 2002: 11) and often does not live up to expectations of private equity investment companies.

Interviewees from the group of institutional private equity investors commented that the quality of a business's management information system is indicative of the quality of a particular business and its employees. Similarly, Koch/Wegmann argue that a large number of chances and risks are reflected in the business's accounting system, controlling reports and financial planning tools and for that reasons are of significant value – in particular in the initial due diligence process (Koch/Wegmann 2002: 39).

Prior to executing an investment institutional private equity investors seek assurance that a close monitoring and controlling of the targeted business is possible ex post. The private equity investor's intention to benchmark financial performance of the targeted business against predefined targets make the existence of a well-functioning management information system indispensable. In addition, since buyout focused private equity investment companies typically do not get involved operationally in their portfolio businesses, a well functioning management information system is necessary to stay informed about the portfolio business's development. In that way the management information system allows the private equity investment company to overview and to keep control of the portfolio business's activities. Next to the private equity investment company's information needs in particular the stringent debt covenants of debt providers ask for a well-functioning information management system.

Accounting data make the backbone of every efficient management information system. A capable accounting department is able to render information about the development of costs and revenues as well as profit development for individual clients respectively business segments, product groups and individual specifications accurately and timely. The accounting department should be able to deliver to management quickly utilizable comparisons of planned to actual performance figures which requires, of course, adequate corporate planning/ budgeting. "The relevance of the accounting department is comparable to the relevance of nautical instruments to determine and monitor course on a ship at sea" (Leopold et al. 2003: 120). In Leopold's words, when management defines the course to follow accounting should be able to report that the business is on track or indicate that adjustments are necessary due to deviation.

However, as was highlighted above, especially small family businesses often do not exhibit organizational structures necessary to support a management information system. Many of these businesses do not generate short-term income statements, budget plans and annual financial statements (much less audited financial statements) due to cost/benefit considerations. Such organizational deficiencies typically imply that the business is unsuitable for consideration by private equity investment companies.

5.2.1.4 Concentrated ownership

According to statements of family business owners, buyout managers and institutional private equity investors the conflict potential within a family business (including the family) is low if ownership is concentrated in one person (single shareholder) with sole leadership- and management responsibility. In contrast, in case of dispersed ownership the conflict potential within the family business multiplies. Characteristic of ownership dispersion in family businesses is the fragmentation of ownership- and voting rights among different family members or -clans.

Interviewed institutional private equity investors pointed out that they have reservations about investing in (private) businesses with dispersed ownership. On one hand transaction costs associated with realizing a MBO/MBI transaction tend to be higher compared to similar transactions involving a single owner. In the case of buyout succession, the literature suggests that the probability of a cooperative MBO/MBI negotiation process is reduced if family firms have dispersed ownership (Axelrod 1980; Fudenberg/Tirole 1991; Cable/Shane 1997). In fact, this also seems to hold true for dispersed governance- and management structures (cp. 4.1.3).

On the other hand, interviewed private equity investors mentioned that private businesses with multiple owners tend to be less well-managed than similar businesses with concentrated ownership, thus generally constituting less attractive investment targets. Similar findings are found in previous studies. E.g. Bergamin expects that only one third of SME businesses with dispersed ownership survive long-term (cp. Bergamin 1995: 35). Strategic decisions of fundamental importance in these businesses typically are difficult to accomplish potentially leading to a fatal deadlock. In context of succession planning this deadlock typically intensifies due to the nature of the decision at hand, i.e. the irreversibility of the decision taken.

5.2.1.5 Conclusion

Family businesses ideally suited for the realization of a private equity backed succession buyout feature (1) stable and predictable cashflows, (2) firm and defendable market positions, (3) organizational structures with clearly confined business units supporting an effective management information system and (4) a concentration of ownership rights in the hands of one or few individual(s).

All of these factors are presumed to be reciprocally implicated. The factor with the strongest influence on other factors appears to be market position. Market leading businesses tend to have an above-average size and are more likely to exhibit functional organizational structures and those types of management information systems expected by institutional private equity investors. However, in view of an increasingly difficult debt financing environment, interviewees ranked stability of cashflows top among requirements towards buyout candidate businesses. The potential for liquidity boosting reorganization of existing business structures thereby assumes a secondary role.

As was discussed above, especially small family businesses often do not exhibit organizational structures necessary to support an efficient management information system. Consequently, business risk and implications of financing succession for the investor become difficult to assess. Further, even though a small business might possess a functional organizational structure, hold an above-average market position and earn high, sustainable cashflows, such a business is unable to accommodate most private equity investment companies' minimum investment requirements.

In conclusion, it appears that medium-sized, economically stable businesses with low or marginal default risk featuring a concentrated ownership structure appear to be most suitable for the realization of a private equity backed succession MBO/MBI.

5.2.2 Expectations towards the external environment

This chapter focuses on external environmental conditions impacting on private equity backed succession buyouts. In particular transaction success is conditioned by the economic-, tax-, legal- and cultural environments discussed subsequently.

5.2.2.1 Economic environment

Interviewees from the group of institutional private equity investors indicated that they favour a solid capital market environment at the time of transaction closure, whereas the capital market environment predominantly is characterized by the stock market environment. Notably all institutional private equity investors described an ideal type transaction environment but rarely made the connection to individual, realized transactions. It can be deduced that buyout focused private equity investment companies principally target strong-growing or otherwise appealing businesses and do not primarily seek to invest in businesses attractively priced due to depressed capital markets. The secondary relevance of the economic environment in influencing investment decisions of private equity investment companies is exemplified in particular by one interviewee's statement:

"We actually search for value in the business and less in the environment. We do not speculate – what other people continue to do – that capital markets circumstances change and that you build value by means of clever financial engineering and a favourable environment or good timing, essentially cycle play." (Institutional private equity investor)

In difference, previous research attributes a high relevance to the trade cycle in influencing investment decisions of private equity investment companies. E.g. Huydts argues that a distinctive disposition factor for the state of the market for private businesses is the trade cycle, in particular the fluctuation of interest rates, stock market prices and foreign exchange rates (Huydts 1992: 179 et sqq.). It should be noted that a low interest rate level not only has positive effects in context of debt financing but is also indicative of difficult macro-economic conditions that generally allow investors to negotiate lower purchase prices (cp. Jakoby 2000: 347). In contrast, with increasing interest rate levels the buying appetite of private equity investment companies diminishes due to the high level of debt that is typically part of the financing structure (cp. chapter 5.1.4.3). On the other hand, purchase prices tend to increase with a rise in interest rates, not least since valuation formulas (such as the DCF method) aim to capture current capital market conditions in their discounting rates.[19] In any case, according to interviewee's statements fears of an enduring recession appear to constitute the largest accountable threat (specific to the economic environment) to transaction success.

Other interviewees from the group of institutional private equity investors indicated that to them solely modest growth of the targeted business's industry sector is the most important factor related to economic environmental conditions. This allows the targeted business to grow without overly battling for market share while comfortably satisfying debt service payments.

At last, another factor influencing an investment decision is the perceived condition of the economic environment at the time of divesture. To some extent private equity investment companies test the future marketability of targeted portfolio investments prior to an investment. As interviewees stated the condition of the "exit environment" at a later point in time, e.g. a favourable stock market condition in case of an aimed for IPO, is also impacting on a private equity investment company's investment decision

5.2.2.2 Tax environment

According to one interviewed institutional private equity investor the tax environment is "the Achilles' heel" of every private equity transaction. According to the assessment of all interviewed private equity investors the German private equity market is suffering from an inconsistent tax policy. A much quoted study of the European Private Equity and Venture Capital Association (EVCA) places Germany third last in an EU-wide benchmarking of tax- and legal framework conditions for company founders and financial investors. In that way Germany ranks behind countries such as Greece, Spain and Portugal (cp. EVCA 2003: 7).

According to one institutional private equity investor most private equity investment companies seek to capitalize on inefficient tax law. Outsiders might think that due to the sheer complexity of German tax law private equity investment companies might have ample opportunity to capitalize on inefficiencies. However, since German tax law is constantly subject to change this becomes increasingly difficult:

19 However, according to Huydts oftentimes average yields of domestic government bonds find application; therefore this effect must be qualified (cp. Huydts 1992: 180 et sq.).

"The greatest challenge is continuous change ... This goes so far that changes come into effect retroactively! We have no planning reliability which certainly impacts on our decision whether or not to invest in Germany ..." (Institutional private equity investor)

"... In the 80's and 90's you had a lot more room for the design of tax shields. Then it was much easier to realize financing structures gentle to cashflow, e.g. step-ups, depreciation potential ..." (Institutional private equity investor)

Interviewees commented that tax law in Germany in international comparison is less friendly to investors than in other jurisdictions. As one interviewee from the group of institutional private equity investors specifically stated, the introduction of the "Zinsschranke" as part of the "Unternehmensteuerreform" in 2008 is considerably impacting on the possibility to finance business acquisitions with debt urging private equity investment companies to dislocate portfolio businesses (or selected parts) to other jurisdictions. For hat reason a dampening of investment activity in Germany further can not be ruled out.

Interviewees from the group of family business owners did not comment on tax issues in any detail. However, family business owners mentioned that tax implications of available succession routes certainly impact on their choice among them. In context of succession buyouts constituting the full disposal of interests in the business subject to the buyout, statements of interviewed family business owners indicate that minimization of inheritance tax burdens is the most pressing tax-related issue pertaining to succession. In consideration of potential tax-related inhibitors to the realization of a succession buyout the important function of tax advisors - not only to acquirers but also to vendors - in the transaction process becomes apparent (cp. chapter 5.1.4.1).

In conclusion, it can be constituted that German taxation schemes are less favourable to (private equity) investors than in other jurisdictions. However, tax issues related to the newly introduced "Unternehmensteuerreform" are not specific to private equity backed succession buyouts but generally affect all investment activity involving debt financing. At the same time, inheritance tax burdens impacting on vendors of family businesses are not specific to private equity backed succession buyout scenarios and also implicated by other succession alternatives. For that reason, from statements of interviewees the tax environment per se was not identified to rank among the most critical factors determining transaction success in private equity backed succession buyouts.

5.2.2.3 Legal environment

In difference to the regulated capital markets (e.g. stock market) the private equity market is not subject to a particularly strong standardization. In that way, the relatively open scopes for the legal design of transactions allow for a customizing towards individual needs of market participants which is generally viewed to be positive by both institutional private equity investors and family business owners.

However, at the same time, one interviewed private equity investor specifically mentioned that the standardization of contract design in private equity backed buyouts still has much potential and is expedient. An increased level of standardization, e.g. as is the case in the trading of receivables (factoring), reduces transaction costs associated with private equity backed succession buyouts and in that way would enervate one of the inhibiting aspects family business owners associate with a private equity backed succession solution (cp. chapter 5.3.3).

Today many developments pertaining to legal standards of private equity investment are spurred by developments in the United States and the United Kingdom. In the United States, for example, the *Delaware Law*, which to a large extent finds use in US corporate law, constitutes so-called fairness standards that dictate a fair conduct of negotiations and a price fixing in the due diligence process (cp. Then Bergh 1998: 29). Interviewed consultants mentioned that the promotion of similar, uniform legal frameworks in Germany would be welcomed insofar as transaction costs for involved parties could be reduced making private equity backed buyouts a more attractive succession route.

5.2.2.4 Cultural environment

The cultural environment has a strong, although subtle effect on realizing a private equity backed succession buyout in Germany. The undifferentiated, oftentimes ill-conceived perception of private equity investment companies in the German public biases family business owner's decision-making when opting for or against a private equity backed succession solution.

Respondents from the group of consultants stated that the esteem of private equity investment companies in the German public continues to be marked by "distrust" and "envy". In particular the "locust debate" in 2004 initiated by SPD chairman Franz Müntefering and the "raider image" attributed to private equity investment companies due to excesses observed in individual private equity sponsored transactions have fuelled such prejudices.

Due to the fact that private equity investors principally operate in the background of their (private) portfolio businesses and out of their self-conception principally avoid publicity, most outsiders are receptive to critical voices. Common allegations circle around the notion that private equity investment companies are exclusively oriented towards short-term results thereby pursuing strategies that maximize their wealth while disregarding other stakeholders.

"Private equity investors create value for their investors but not for my employees." (Family business owner)

Among recent investment cases allegedly confirming such recriminations are e.g. the buyout of automotive supplier Kiekert by a consortium of funds advised by Permira and KKR in 2000, the buyout of fittings maker Grohe in 2004 by funds advised by a TPG-led consortium, or the buyout of Tank and Rast in 2004 by a fund advised by Terra Firma. Among other issues, all of these transactions struggled under an overly heavy debt burden. Unsurprisingly, one interviewee from the group of institutional private equity investors mentioned that overleveraging in context of a buyout is among the greatest threats to long-term success of such transactions (cp. also chapter 5.2.2.4).

However, one interviewed consultant observed that the following circumstance is often ignored: Many businesses seeking and receiving private equity financing are in need of restructuring. Since restructuring cases are more difficult than non-restructuring cases from a managerial point of view and therefore make challenging investment cases, many of these businesses fail - despite and not due to the private equity investor's involvement.

As became apparent from conducted interviews, deep-rooted misconceptions also circle around the issue of whether private equity investment companies are able to achieve surpluses and how possible surpluses are distributed. In this context one interviewed institutional private equity investor mentioned that ultimately investors hold a private equity investment company accountable for achieving high returns on entrusted monies.

"Many people do not understand that we have a custody duty towards our investors. And among those are also pension funds that mandate us with the investment of retirement provisions of common employees ..." (Institutional private equity investor)

Recent initiatives of industry associations and practitioners as well as increasingly differentiated media coverage have put positive aspects of institutional private equity to the fore. A more differentiated appraisal of private equity investment companies then is typically found among the younger rather than the older generation of family business owners (cp. Reimers 2004: 32). Consultants interviewed also mentioned that unprejudiced family business owners typically at least also credit private equity investment companies with assuming an economically meaningful ("efficiency-boosting") role. Those that hold a more in-depth understanding typically acknowledge the contribution of private equity investment companies to accelerate necessary change processes in their portfolio businesses.

Besides manifold misconceptions due to a lack of public relations efforts of private equity investment companies coupled with predominantly unfavourable media coverage, incomprehension is also caused by the "different languages" spoken by institutional private equity investors and family business owners. As discussed earlier in this study, soft factors are likely to exacerbate an approach by either party (cp. chapter 5.1.1.1 and 5.1.2.1).

On the other hand, although the cultural framework conditions for private equity investment companies in Germany are less favourable than in other countries such as the United States or the United Kingdom, the "cultural environment" is unlikely to cause private equity investment companies to cease investment in succession buyouts in Germany. As interviewees from the group of institutional private equity investors repeatedly expressed, many German family businesses are highly esteemed internationally and make very attractive acquisition targets ("hidden champions").

5.2.2.5 Conclusion

In context of private equity backed succession buyouts it can be concluded that the conditions of the current and expected future state of the economic-, legal- and tax environment impacts on the private equity investment company's investment decision as well as the buyout managers' decision to undertake the buyout. As long as the vendor's decision for business divesture via a private equity backed MBO/MBI is not forced upon him/her, the same holds true for the vendor.

Among all external environmental factors discussed in this chapter the cultural environment has the strongest effect on family business owners making a decision for or against a private equity backed succession buyout, as statements of interviewees consistently indicate. If sufficiently unfavourable, the cultural environment must be viewed as a strong inhibitor to the realization of such succession route.

5.3 Transaction process

As highlighted in chapter 3.2, the private equity backed succession buyout process is characterized by transaction costs attributable to information asymmetries between contract partners. This chapter analyzes and discusses transaction costs occurring in private equity backed succession buyouts due to the involvement of a private equity investment company. In other words, this chapter highlights transaction costs induced by a private equity investment company. This perspective of analysis was chosen to accommodate the circumstance that divestment processes in context of realizing succession are principally initiated by existing owners and that the owner ultimately is responsible for determining the succession route.[20] Transaction costs occurring due to contractual agreements between private equity investment companies and buyout managers (ex ante or ex post) are not focus of discussion and largely ignored.

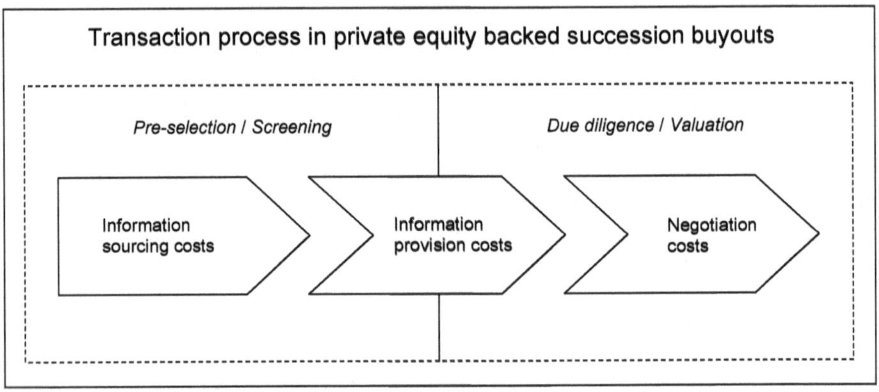

Figure 29: Transaction process in PE backed succession buyouts.
Source: Author's illustration.

Following the subdivision of transaction costs introduced in chapter 3.2, this chapter separately discusses information sourcing costs (chapter 5.3.1), information provision costs (chapter 5.3.2) and negotiation costs (chapter 5.3.3).

20 It should be stated that buyout managers are confronted with the same type of costs as family business owners, however, potentially in different scope.

5.3.1 Information sourcing costs

This chapter analyzes and discusses information sourcing costs induced by a family business owner's intention to realize a private equity backed succession buyout.

5.3.1.1 Character of information sourcing costs

Preceding considerations of information sourcing costs accumulating on the side of family business owners when considering a private equity backed succession buyout, it is necessary to mention that an elementary precondition for the realization of a private equity backed succession buyout is the acknowledgement of the existence of such a succession alternative. As an earlier chapter highlighted (cp. chapter 5.1.1.1), family business owners in Germany remain largely unaware of private equity financing options. Accordingly, private equity is not much used in the financing mix of German family businesses.

If the existence of a private equity backed succession alternative is acknowledged, family business owners typically seek detailed knowledge about the private equity market and its suppliers. In practice, however, exactly this knowledge is considerably underdeveloped. Conducted interviews revealed considerable information deficiencies among family business owners pertaining to the private equity market in general and the opportunity to realize succession via a private equity backed buyout in particular.

In the course of identifying a suitable private equity partner, family business owners are challenged to answer the following questions: (1) Which sources of private equity exist? (2) Which private equity investment companies are active in Germany? (3) Which private equity investment company is most suitable to finance the intended transaction? (4) How can pre-selected private equity investors be contacted and which information do they require?

Finding an answer to each question necessarily is associated with specific information sourcing costs. A fundamental precondition for the occurrence of these costs is that the vendor has freedom of choice with regard to the succession route and with regard to selecting among different providers of private equity capital. Only in those cases information search activity and information search costs occur.

The scope of information sourcing costs essentially is contingent on the transparency of the private equity market. The more transparent a particular market (segment), the easier and more cost-efficient is the answering of market specific questions (cp. Albach 1991: 267).[21] The rate of transparency of a market foremost corresponds with the degree of organization, level of publicity as well as extent of information asymmetry among market participants.

5.3.1.2 Determinants of information sourcing costs

Degree of organization: Differences in the accruement of costs associated with sourcing information about private equity investment companies occur if the degree of organization of individual market segments differs. The degree of organization can be understood to be the extent of the integration of individual private equity companies within one segment; in practice, for example, central points of information, trade associations or geographical networks of private equity investment companies.[22] In Germany especially the BVK offers a fairly comprehensive overview of the German private equity market, communicates selected rough criteria for pre-selection such as industry focus and financing stage and provides contact details of associated members.

Depth and credibility of information: The degree of organization of a market (segment) principally determines the degree of costs associated with the procurement of a general market overview. However, costs associated with the assessment of individual market participants (i.e. private equity investment companies) remain largely unaffected. Private equity investment companies make use of different measures to disclose information about themselves including maintaining an internet (website) presence, publishing and disseminating information brochures or the participation in road- or tradeshows. However, it can be assumed that all private equity investment companies have a considerable interest in representing information and characteristics relevant to sourcing investment opportunities as positive as possible. Next to the depth of information provided it is also the credibility of such information that appears to be of critical relevance (cp. also chapter 5.1.2.1).

Existence of multipliers: Chapter 5.1.4 highlighted contributions of consultants and other financial intermediaries to the transaction process. Consultants and other financial intermediaries play a critical role in reducing information sourcing costs for family business owners in context of private equity backed succession buyouts. Private equity investment companies with a sufficient reputation

---

21 In line with findings in chapter 5.1.1.1, information sourcing costs are reduced if the family business owner has had prior experience with institutional private equity.

22 The majority of German private equity investment companies are associated with the *Bundesverband deutscher Kapitalbeteiligungsgesellschaften* (BVK).

in the private equity market are able to source investment opportunities directly, respectively are directly approached by businesses seeking financing. However, a good name as a sole pillar of marketing appears to be insufficient for the majority of (small and medium-sized) private equity investment companies. Although private equity investment companies may use different channels of media communication to market their financing services, marketing measures such as advertisements typically create not much more than a PR effect. The reason being that the vast majority of addressed businesses do not have demand for financing (e.g. a succession buyout) at the time of publication.

For this reason successful private equity investment companies principally source investment opportunities by means of a network of *multipliers* that hold or may acquire information about businesses seeking equity financing. Foremost, these multipliers appear to be (local) banks, i.e. the "house banks" of businesses seeking equity financing as well as consultants counselling businesses in such matters as corporate finance, tax- and legal issues as well as issues pertaining to annual audits (cp. chapter 5.1.4.1). More recently, also industry associations as well as chambers of commerce can be counted among the multipliers for private equity investment companies (Leopold et al. 2003: 150). Not last, as statements from interviewees from the group of institutional private equity investors indicate, networks among private equity investment companies often lead to referrals of investment opportunities or opportunities to syndicate investments.

It can be assumed that a network of regional branch offices furthers the development of contacts to relevant multipliers. This proposition corresponds with the demand of interviewed family business owners for "regional connectivity" of private equity investment companies (cp. chapter 5.1.2.2). Key is how systematic and frequent contacts within the private equity investment company's network are nourished. In particular information dissemination about interesting, successfully closed transactions have a lasting effect on multipliers as can be deduced from statements of interviewed consultants. In this context the standard "nothing succeeds more than success" comes into one's own (cp. chapter 5.1.2.2). Multipliers that learn about successful transactions are likely to be "programmed" to give their business clients according reference (Leopold et al. 2003: 151). The disclosure of details pertaining to past transactions builds the basis for an examination of a private equity investment company's reputation and, in addition, equally builds trust among multipliers and (potential) vendors of businesses.

5.3.2 Information provision costs

This chapter analyzes and discusses information provision costs induced by the private equity investment company in the course of realizing a private equity backed succession buyout.

5.3.2.1 Character of information provision costs

In the run-up of a private equity backed succession buyout it is not only the family business owner seeking information about the private equity investment company and the buyout management team but also the private equity investment company seeking detailed information about the investment opportunity and its potential contract partners. Within the scope of this assessment costs on the side of the targeted family business occur. Accordingly, the second group of costs comprises those expenditures caused by the private equity investment company's information needs prior to making an investment decision. The process towards the investment decision principally can be split in the two phases *pre-selection/screening* and *due diligence/valuation* (cp. Wright/Robbie 1998: 535). In both phases specific costs of information provision induced by the private equity investment company occur.

The private equity investment company's *pre-selection/screening* of investment opportunities typically occurs on basis of submitted business plans (cp. chapter 5.1.3.4). Next to the allocation of management resources potentially also costs associated with the procurement of market information accrue in assembling the business plan.[23] Expenditures during the phase of *due diligence* may be split in direct and indirect costs. Direct costs occur immediately in the interaction between the family business owner, the buyout management team and the private equity investment company and the sourcing and allocation of requested information. Indirect costs occur in the origination of signals aimed to convey attractiveness of the targeted business and the operability of the transaction to the private equity investment company. After a first positive assessment of the business plan, institutional private equity investors typically seek to establish a personal contact followed by a more detailed analysis as part of the due diligence phase. Finally, cumulated information is used for the *valuation* of the business

23 However, these costs may not comprehensively attributed to information provision costs. The business plan has – next to making the business's potential for external capital providers more transparent – also the purpose of allowing management and owners a better assessment of the business's chances and risks. Further, the business plan might be used as a controlling tool for recurring performance review.

building the basis for actual negotiation. Next to the costs mentioned, opportunity costs may arise due to the duration of the due diligence- and valuation phase. If both phases protract over an extended period of time, the succession process and/or the business's operations are impaired.

5.3.2.2 Determinants of information provision costs

Level of initiative and quality of provided information: The extent of information provision costs is essentially contingent on the scope of the private equity investment company's information needs. A result of adverse selection (i.e. the financing of a MBO/MBI that, ex post, appears to be unworthy of financing) is the deterioration of the average profit situation of the private equity investment company. In this sense the private equity investment company has a heightened interest in avoiding the problem of adverse selection. The more initiative potential contract partners generate in reducing existing information asymmetries, the fewer are information requests by the private equity investment company. Consequently, information provision costs for the family business might decrease.

However, even without the intention to conceal information that could have a disadvantageous effect on valuation, the family business owner has a legitimate interest to not let potential acquirers look too deeply into the economic situation of the business. The private equity investment company's due diligence for that reason has its natural boundaries in the willingness of the vendor to allow the associated sourcing of information. Background of the vendor's apprehension to provide business internals to potential acquirers commonly is the fear that a sales-/purchase agreement in the end will not materialize. The *nondisclosure interests* of the vendor are best served if the vendor only then discloses information when sufficiently certain that a sales-/purchase agreement is realizable and does not cease to exist at a later point in time (cp. Holzapfel/Pöllath 2000: 17). Then, however, vendors typically seek to lavish acquirers with information in order to eliminate or curtail potential warranty claims ex post as interviewed consultants observed.

Level of trust between potential contract partners: However, the divergence of interests between potentially contracting parties is not insurmountable. The vendor equally has an interest in receiving a substantiated purchase offer and seeks to give a potential acquirer preferably few reasons to degrade the offer at a later point in time due to new information (cp. Holzapfel/Pöllath 2000: 33 et sq.). At the same time a potential acquirer, although obliged to obtain all information relevant to pricing the business, is also interested to not alienate the vendor by untimely audits including long questionnaires, brigades of auditors, etc. The irritations caused on the side of vendors by such investigation very early in the process appear to be an effective barrier to transaction success as interviewed consultants indicated. In this context the critical importance of trust and the establishment of a trustful relationship to the vendor is, again, accentuated (cp. chapter 5.1.2.1). Only those institutional private equity investors able to win the trust of the vendor succeed in sourcing information indispensable to initiating substantiated negotiation talks.

Expertise and experience of private equity investment companies: Another lever for the reduction of information asymmetries is the efficiency of screening- and due diligence measures employed. The screening exemplifies the private equity investment company's procurement of information during the pre-selection phase but also the accumulation of more generic market (segment) information. Objective here is the observation of characteristics associated with the targeted business and the business's market that lead to a meaningful assessment of the business's development potential (cp. Perridon/Steiner 1993: 522). The private equity investment company's screening and due diligence competence essentially determines the quality of the assessment of the investment's potential. One possibility to optimize the private equity investment company's screening- and due diligence effectiveness is in the *specialization* on defined industry segments, financing stages and types of targeted businesses etc. Next to specialization, also *size* and in particular *experience* exemplified in the number of successfully closed transactions and tenure of market presence, are indicative of screening- and due diligence competence. Finally, the quality of the private equity investment company's *network* in the market impacts on the level of screening- and due diligence competence. The more experienced a private equity investor, the easier the accurate assessment of investment opportunities. For that reason, the investment return (i.e. the internal rate of return (IRR)) achieved on past investments gives a reliable indication of the private equity investment company's screening- and due diligence competence.[24]

Relinquishment of syndication: Statements of interviewed consultants indicate that the involvement of multiple private equity investment companies tends to impede the transaction process. Information provision costs are confined to costs attributable to the interaction with potential contract partners and the origination of positive signals. If a private equity investment company is not able to accommodate the full amount of financing needed to realize a succession buyout, this does not have considerable effects on the second group of costs. Since costs for the origination of signals, be they in form of the composition of a business

24 A detailed discussion on the IRR as a benchmark for success offers Schefczyk 2000: 154 et sqq.

plan or the assembling of a management team, already occur for the first private equity investment company, no additional costs accrue in co-investment scenarios comprising multiple investors. However, this is different for the first group of costs: The interaction with any additional private equity investment company binds additional management resources and -time and therefore is associated with additional transaction costs. In exclusive consideration of these arguments those private equity investment companies are to be favoured that are able to fully finance the succession MBO/MBI in conjunction with buyout managers.

5.3.3 Negotiation costs

Chapter 5.3.3 analyzes and discusses negotiation costs induced by the private equity investment company in the course of realizing a private equity backed succession buyout.

5.3.3.1 Characteristics of negotiation costs

The category of negation costs comprises all those expenditures related to actual contract negotiations and -design. After closing of the private equity investment company's due diligence phase, potential contract partners engage in negotiations about the explicit and legally binding form of the sales-/purchase contract. Costs occurring in this phase can be split in two categories. On one hand direct costs associated with the form of and agreement on contractual agreements accumulate; on the other hand opportunity costs occur caused by abandoning negotiations at a late stage and by configuring the contract's constituent parts.

Direct costs associated with contract negotiations predominantly accrue in form of labor costs, in particular the provision of management resources. Due to the prominence and far- reaching consequences of arrangements subject to contracting, negotiations are rarely delegated but rather conducted personally by the family business owner and buyout managers as interviewees underscored.

Next to direct costs, indirect costs related to the length of negotiation and contract configuration accrue. Noteworthy here are already pointed to costs of a protracted succession process with potentially damaging effects for the business and the business's stakeholders (cp. chapter 5.3.2). Also, negotiation outcomes disadvantageous for the family business owner, buyout managers or the targeted business and its stakeholders principally must be associated with costs. In addition, interviewed institutional private equity investors confirmed that they typically demand exclusivity from potential contract partners at this stage of the transaction process. For that reason, negotiators acting on behalf of the targeted family business often are barred from conducting additional, parallel negotiation talks with other potential investors.

5.3.3.2 Determinants of negotiation costs

Level of trust between potential contract partners: In consideration of the manifold contract components and agreement options it becomes obvious that a sales-/purchase agreement typically assumes high complexity and thus high transaction costs occur. Nevertheless, contract partners are not able to close exhaustive contracts specifying accurately all services and return services and anticipating all possible contingencies ex post (cp. Jost 2000: 223). In fact, due to bounded rationality of potential contract partners, the limited measurability of services subject to exchange and the persistence of information asymmetries, a sales-/purchase contract must always remain incomplete. Necessarily contractual gaps arise that might not be possible to sanctify judicially ex post. To that extent the need for a trustful, transaction costs-reducing relationship between vendor and acquirer is again accentuated at this stage of the transaction process (cp. chapters 5.1.1.1 and 5.1.2.1).

Expertise and experience of contract partners: That the level of expertise and experience of individuals involved in negotiations directly affects the duration of the negotiation process is self-evident. The more often sales-/purchase contracts were closed, the less the insecurity about the effectiveness of contractual conditions and the implications ex post. However, as was discussed in chapter 5.1.1.2, to most family business owners business divesture constitutes a first- and one-time experience. For that reason, the technical expertise and experience of individuals acting on behalf of the private equity investment company is of critical relevance and a good indicator of the investor's ability to appropriately organize the negotiation process and the configuration of contractual agreements. Attributes such as the number of closed transactions and the tenure in the private equity market are indicative of the seniority and professionalism of individual private equity investors. High transaction costs accrue in informal- and rather unprofessionally managed negotiation processes without a stringent time schedule (cp. Achleitner et al. 2008: 31). In addition, professionalism finally is associated with the use of ready-made standard agreements in particular contractual situations (cp. chapter 5.2.2.2). Thereby time for the configuration of contractual agreements and thus transaction costs can be reduced.

Reputation of the private equity investment company: As discussed in chapter 5.1.2.2, the private equity investment company's track record (of realized investments) is indicative of the investor's behavior during a particular investment's holding period. Private equity investment companies that publish information pertaining to previously completed investments offer a basis for a verification of their reputation and build confidence among potential contract partners. However, as interviewees from the group of consultants explained, also if no extensive track record (and no basis for the investor's reputation) is existent, indicators of the investor's reliability may exist. E.g. especially private equity investment companies associated with or owned by larger financial institutions that run the risk of damaging the reputation of associated (parent) organizations tend to be reliable market participants.

Degree of objective divergence of potential contract partners: The extent of objective divergence between the departing family business owner and the private equity investment company can be counted among the most relevant determinants of transaction costs in the negotiation phase. In this context a differentiation of *short-* and *long-term objectives* of potential contract partners is feasible.

Divergence in *short-term objectives* in the form of sales price maximization, respectively purchase price minimization, inevitably induces costs in the negotiation phase. As interviewees from the group of institutional private equity investors stated, among the classical psychological negotiation faults on the side of vendors is to initiate negotiation processes with highly inflated price expectations (cp. chapter 5.1.1.3). The motive of vendors often is the rather misleading hope to open up negotiation leeway. From the perspective of the private equity investment company this implies the necessity to depress the valuation to such an extent that a substantial draw back from the initially stipulated valuation might still make an advantageous result for the vendor. However, experienced investors look through this approach and perceive it to be dishonourable. This may result in a deterioration of previously built up trust which, in turn, may cause the accruement of additional transaction costs or, potentially, the abortion of negotiation talks. As interviewees from the group of institutional private equity investors mentioned, the maxim for negotiation rather must be to name realistic terms for all integral parts of the sales-/purchase contract and to justify these consistently and logically. Also in the realm of realistic valuations substantial bandwidth for negotiation typically remains. In the case of working with realistic valuations the vendor does not run the risk of loosing face for first "trying to pull a fast one on the other side" as one interviewed consultant commented. Guiding principle pertaining to the conduct of negotiations should be openness and the conveyance of trustworthiness among potential contract partners as if already definitely contract partners (cp. chapter 5.1.2.1). The EVCA found that over half (53 percent) of respondents in their survey on private equity backed succession buyouts reported that the sale price was mutually agreed on by acquirers and vendors, pointing to a balanced negotiation process. More than a quarter of respondents stated that the vendor proposed a fixed price that maximized his/her valuation (27 percent), although 11 percent felt that the fixed price proposed by the vendor was fair and adequate (EVCA 2005: 15).

In context of *long-term objectives* of potential contract partners it can be stated that the more potential contract partners' objectives and ideas in realizing contractual agreements harmonize, the earlier an agreement is achievable and the less the risk of breach of promises ex post. This implies that imperfect contracts not anticipating all possible actions and reactions of contract partners ex post may be closed. Here again the direct impact of the level of social compatibility between the family business owner and the private equity investor on the scope of negotiation costs occurring becomes apparent (cp. chapter 5.1.2.1). Which long-term objectives of the private equity investor further the reduction of complexity pertaining to the sales-/purchase contract can principally not be discussed without the advertence of individual objectives of the departing family business owner. However, as discussed previously, among the central objectives of most family business owners confronted with succession is the long-term perpetuation of the family business. Thus it appears that private equity investment companies able to credibly signal the intention to sponsor and support businesses for an extended period of time principally reduce the occurrence of negation costs.

5.3.4 Conclusion

A transaction cost framework was used to highlight the extent of frictions arising in context of the private equity backed succession buyout process. The discussion in this chapter built on the theoretical foundations presented in chapter 3.2. It was shown that the likelihood of achieving transaction success increases proportionally to the reduction of transaction costs induced by the private equity investment company. Only if information sourcing-, information provision- and negotiation costs for the vendor are sufficiently low - i.e. not considerably higher than for other succession alternatives - transaction success is realizable.

Due to the lack of both transparency and organization of the private equity market, *information search costs* for potential transaction partners are considerably high. While private equity investment companies are specialized on identifying-, screening- and conducting due diligence on investment opportunities, the search for a suitable private equity investor constitutes a first- and one time experience to most family business owners. It appears that initially family business owner's information needs circle around the reduction of information deficiencies pertaining institutional private equity and possible arrangement alternatives for private equity backed succession. Only subsequently a pointed search for a private equity investment company fitting the departing owner's succession needs might follow.

With regard to *information provision costs*, family business owners largely appear to be unprepared in meeting the information needs of institutional private equity investors. For that reason the extent of information provision costs essentially is contingent on the investor's effectiveness in sourcing- and assessing information. Although information provision costs induced by a private equity investment company are considerable, it is questionable if these costs are higher relative to costs induced by other types of investors, e.g. strategic investors. If syndication of the equity investment can be avoided, the occurrence of information provision costs is curtailed to the information needs of a single investor.

The extent of *negotiation costs* occurring also principally is contingent on the institutional private equity investor's expertise and experience. In addition, the alignability of potential contract partners' objectives determines the duration of negotiations and the scope of negotiation costs occurring. Accordingly, the more short-term objectives (i.e. expectations on sales-/purchase price) and long-term objectives (i.e. expectations circling around the targeted business's future) of potential contract partners deviate, the more extensive the occurrence of negotiation costs.

6 Conclusions and outlook

In this study an interview research design was developed on basis of Kern's interaction theory. On this base 18 expert interviews were conducted, transcribed and analyzed. Empirical findings in this study were contrasted and supplemented with findings of previous, related research. This approach delivered insights with high practical value for those parties principally involved in private equity backed succession buyouts. The subsequent chapters highlight and delimit the central findings of this research (chapter 6.1), discuss implications (chapter 6.2) and limitations (chapter 6.3) of the study, offer suggestions for continuative research in the area (chapter 6.4) and conclude with a brief topical outlook (chapter 6.5).

6.1 Summary of findings

The search for success factors in private equity backed succession buyouts in German family businesses focused on three distinctive dimensions, including the "parties involved", the "framework conditions" and the "transaction process". A synopsis of these dimensions and the success potentials constituting these dimensions are illustrated in figure 30.

The focus of analysis was put on the directly involved. Correspondingly, this dimension is located in the center of figure 30. The author opted to emphasize this dimension since the directly involved appear to have the most immediate effect on the success and failure of private equity backed succession buyouts relative to factors underlying both other dimensions located at the peripheral areas of the illustrated figure. The arrangement of success factors within individual subchapters of chapter 5 marked the relative importance of success factors discussed therein, i.e. more critical success factors were ranked higher in the sequence of discussion than less important ones.

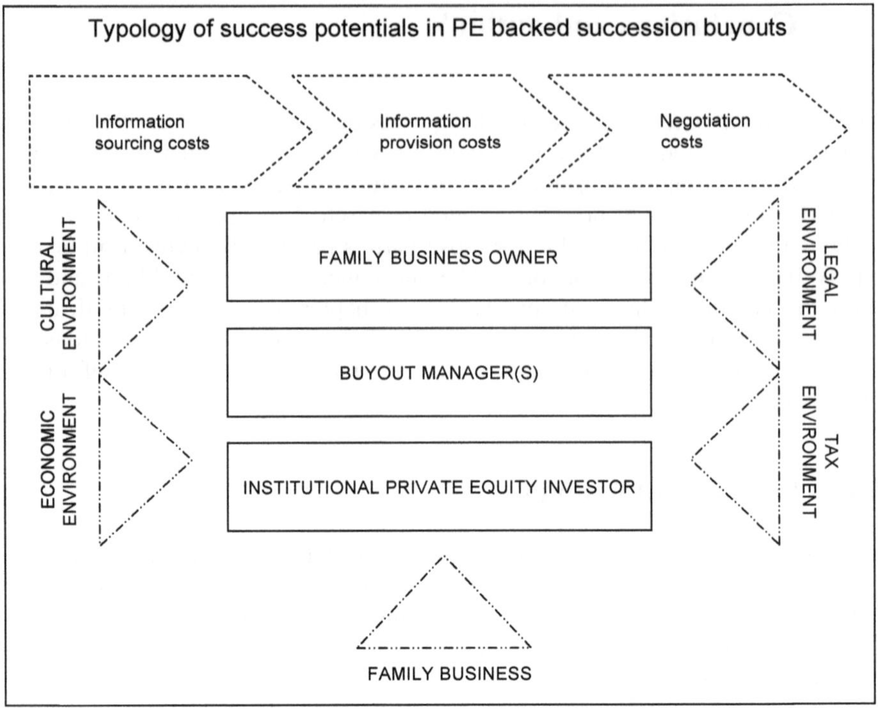

Figure 30: Typology of success potentials.
Source: Author's illustration.

For the identified critical success factors and additional factors impacting on transaction success in reality it must be acknowledged that the specification (even existence or non-existence) of a factor is influenced by the specification of other factors. For example, it must be assumed that a particularly low purchase price of a business can compensate unfavourable specifications of other factors such as factors associated with the economic environment. A rigid catalogue of success factors from a theoretical perspective therefore is inconceivable. However, results of the empirical study show that a number of factors attributable to the involved, the framework conditions and the transaction process are pronounced in successful transactions. It can be assumed, therefore, that the specification of these factors is critically relevant to realizing transaction success. At least it is conceivable that the identified critical success factors were repeatedly noticed empirically due to their pronounced contribution to the overcoming of possible realization constraints.

The following section summarizes the study's main findings in view of the most relevant realization constraints. These constraints directly build on negative specifications of success factors identified, systematized and discussed in chapter 5.

A first group of realization constraints is attributable to the *parties involved*:

(1) Cultural incompatibility between institutional private equity investors and family business owners: The analysis of interviews shows that the preconditions for relationship building between representatives of private equity investment companies and family business owners are principally difficult. Prejudices on both sides hamper relationship building and the establishment of mutual trust. Institutional private equity investors often consider family business owners to be "unworldly" and to be "behind the times". Family business owners, on the other side, oftentimes associate "arrogance", "greed" and "ruthlessness" with institutional private equity investors. In addition, the cultural rift is manifested in communication (i.e. language), mindset and demeanour. These differences quickly come to the fore in succession processes that are highly emotional for the majority of family business owners.

(2) Incompatibility of objectives of private equity investment companies and family business owners: Detached from preferences pertaining to the specification of individual succession routes for the vast majority of departing family business owners premier objective is the long-term perpetuation of the business organization subject to succession. Statements of interviewed family business owners revealed that private equity investment companies with a long-term investment horizon and a customized investment approach closely fitting the needs of value-based family business owners are most likely to be received well among owners and other stakeholders of medium-sized family businesses. However, only few institutional private equity investors fitting these criteria exist.

(3) Lack of suitability of buyout managers: The study's results confirmed the high relevance of management quality for transaction success in private equity backed succession buyouts. While the buyout management team will only be able to prove its managerial qualities ex post, doubts associated with buyout managers' ability to effectively realize the buyout operationally ex post are among the most central factors inhibiting transaction success. While demands with regard to formal qualification, experience and risk-affinity must be regarded as basic prerequisites of buyout managers, ample motivation, stability and long-term commitment of buyout managers appear to be the distinctive attributes affecting transaction success and failure.

(4) Insufficient involvement of specialized external expertise: It clearly emerged that a professional and timely realization of a private equity backed succession buyout is not possible without the support of specialized consultants. Next to the mere technical expertise of consultants nonexistent among institutional private equity investors, family business owners or buyout managers, consultants assume an important catalytic function in the transaction process. The study's as well as other empirical findings indicate that the involvement of consultants tends to reduce frictions among the principally involved by facilitating factual, unemotional dialogue.

A second group of realization constraints is attributable to the *framework conditions:*

(5) Structural deficiencies of the buyout candidate business: Answers from interview partners punctuate that businesses exhibiting a substandard market position principally make unattractive investment targets for buyout focused private equity investment companies. Otherwise, market leading businesses tend to have an above-average size and are more likely to exhibit functional organizational structures and effective management information systems corresponding with institutional private equity investors' expectations. Market leading businesses typically also feature stable and predictable cashflows, the factor ranking top among private equity investors' requirements towards buyout candidate businesses. In addition, medium-sized family businesses with a concentrated ownership structure appear to be most suitable for the realization of a private equity backed succession MBO/MBI.

(6) Insufficient attractiveness of external environmental conditions: Findings indicate that changes in the economic, legal and tax environment considerably affect investment decisions of private equity investment companies. However, it was found that well-run businesses make attractive investment targets for private equity investment companies during most economic conditions and in most of regulatory environments. On the side of family business owners, factors attributable to the cultural environment emerged as most potent in inhibiting success of private equity backed succession buyouts in family businesses. The undifferentiated, oftentimes ill-conceived perception of private equity investment companies in the German public considerably biases family business owners' decision-making when opting for or against a private equity backed succession solution.

Finally, a third group of realization constraints is attributable to the *transaction process:*

(7) High transaction costs for contracting partners: Findings indicate that high transaction costs induced by contracting with a private equity investment company pose a considerable threat to the realization of a private equity backed succession buyout. Thus, the likelihood of achieving transaction success increases proportionally to the reduction of transaction costs induced by the private equity investment company. Only if information sourcing-, information provision- and negotiation costs for the vendor are sufficiently low - i.e. not considerably higher than for other succession alternatives - transaction success is realizable. In particular the extent of negotiation costs occurring is principally contingent on the institutional private equity investor's expertise and experience. In addition, the alignability of potential contract partners' objectives determines the duration of negotiations and the scope of negotiation costs accruing.

In view of an ostensible plethora of issues *opposing* the realization of private equity backed succession buyouts in German family businesses, it is also necessary to reiterate that succession buyouts currently account for approximately a quarter of all succession cases among German family business. It must be assumed that a considerable portion of these succession transactions are (partially) sponsored by institutional private equity investors. In this way, private equity investment companies already assume an important function in the German family business landscape. Considering on one hand that intergenerational succession in family businesses has a tendency to decline further while the relatively young private equity market in Germany is poised to expand in size and scope, the potential for additional growth private equity backed succession buyouts have in Germany becomes evident.

At last it is necessary to point to the outstanding, necessary validation of the qualitative explorative findings summarized in this chapter. Although formulated findings convey an explanatory power with high practical relevance, these can only be regarded as tendency explanations for transaction success respectively transaction failure. In that way, results may not be generalized without further conformational studies. If the formulated findings are reduced to their elementary scientific content, these could be used as prepositions or hypotheses and thus as a basis for quantitative-conformational studies for future research (cp. chapter 6.4).

6.2 Implications

This study delivers additional building blocks for the theoretically orientated research on family business succession, in particular research circling around non-family succession routes. The study's findings also have direct practical relevance for practitioners in the field. More specifically, this study contributes in the following ways.

First, this research constitutes the first comprehensive study of private equity backed succession buyouts in medium-sized German family businesses. The study's approach is unique in that it incorporates three different dimensions in its analysis of factors determining transaction success. The study identified and validated these success factors by administering semi-structured interviews to representatives of groups principally involved in the transaction process, including family business owners, institutional private equity investors, buyout managers and specialized consultants. The author thereby made use of the method of data triangulation. This approach repeatedly pointed to the "clash of cultures" manifested in the distinctive differences between family business owners and institutional private equity investors that was not fully accounted for in earlier studies.

Further, this study ordered and ranked identified success factors according to their relative influence on transaction success. A hierarchy of success factors allows researchers and practitioners equally to scrutinize and prioritize their attention when dealing with private equity backed succession buyouts.

Second, the study contributes to the academic discussion in objectifying the emotionally charged succession process involving institutional private equity. Despite the persistence of prejudices and misconceptions about institutional private equity among family business owners academia generally has accepted that institutional private equity rather has advantageous than disadvantageous effects from an economic point of view. With this study the author hopes to encourage family business owners to view a private equity backed succession buyout as a means to critically examine the viability- and development potential of the family business in its environment, to consider options of repositioning and to implement necessary changes. Experienced private equity investors in many incidences are well positioned to assess if "bottleneck factors" particular to the family business - management capacity, equity capital resources, as well as business size - are compatible with the demands of long-term competitiveness. In that respect many MBOs/MBIs in Germany do not merely constitute transactions facilitating ownership change. Previous empirical findings introduced in chapter 1.3 rather indicate that the MBO/MBI is an effective instrument for the new dynamization of medium-sized family businesses whose verve for growth have softened under leadership of preceding proprietors.

A more rational approach to private equity backed succession buyouts is beneficial to all principally involved parties and, of course, the targeted business's stakeholders. In particular, a gain in knowledge about the expectations and needs of constitutive parties in the private equity backed succession process allows the involved to make informed decisions under which conditions their participation is expedient and leading to desired results.

Third, the study is relevant to practitioners in the field, foremost family business owners faced with succession and private equity investors focusing on investments in the German "Mittelstand". Next to elucidating the issue at hand to an alleged large group of unprepared family business owners, the study should also encourage more private equity investment companies to consider succession buyouts in medium-sized family businesses as viable investment opportunities. Due to the pyramid-like dispersion of businesses in the SME segment buyout focused private equity investment companies are likely to be disappointed by the number of large investment opportunities and overwhelmed by the number of small-sized investment opportunities within the German business landscape. At the same time, it appears that succession buyouts especially among the businesses at the lower end of the spectrum of business sizes are a sought after form of organizing succession. The analysis of empirical data in this study suggests a mismatch of demand and supply of institutional private equity to finance succession buyouts in Germany. While the demand of small family businesses (annual turnover < EUR 50 million) for institutional private equity financing of succession buyouts appears to be insufficiently met, an overhang of capital on the supply side for few, large family businesses with leading market positions exists.

Another most obvious mismatch circles around the divergence of objectives of family business owners and buyout managers on one side and private equity investment companies on the other. Since the limited investment horizon of private equity investment companies principally runs counter to the long-term orientation of both existing family business owners and buyout managers, private equity-type investment companies with long-term investment horizons appear well positioned to better serve the needs of family business owners seeking retirement and buyout managers seeking entrepreneurial independence. For example, the publicly listed investment companies Indus AG, Gesco Holding AG or Greiffenberger AG invest equity capital in succession buyouts of medium-sized German businesses. These investment companies principally have an infinite investment horizon and seek controlling interests in medium-sized, family-owned businesses faced with succession. In addition, these investors offer continued entrepreneurial independence to their portfolio businesses under the patronage of a strong financial partner. However, unlike typical private equity investment companies, these investors are not exit-driven; their business model instead is built on recurring dividend distributions of portfolio businesses. For that reason, such investment strategies do not fit the more narrow definition of the terms "private equity" and "private equity investment company". Nevertheless, empirical findings in this study indicate that demand for such specialized equity investors with holding character will facilitate their acceptation and further their proliferation.

At last, the study's results also add to the discussion on the financing environment of the German 'Mittelstand' in general. The German financial system is in a state of principal change towards a more pronounced market orientation; financing instruments based on capital markets and institutional investors are gaining in importance (Sachverständigenrat 2005: 455). Thus demands towards SME are rising, in particular with regard to management bodies, governance structures and transparency. In principal, this development should be beneficiary to the efficiency of the German financial system. Nevertheless, a great number of German SME perceive the changing financing environment increasingly hostile since the changing banking policy tends to limit the traditional access to financing instruments in form of debt. In Germany the New Basel Capital Accord (Basel II) has become effective at the beginning of 2006 and is expected to be fully implemented in the course of 2009. This accord includes elevated supervision and transparency standards for European banks and in particular requires banks to relate their regulatory equity capital to the risk profile of their credit portfolio and therefore ultimately to the risk profile of borrowers. This demands stringent credit ratings of every borrower and will complicate access to bank loans. In this changing environment the weak equity structure of many German family businesses is becoming the Achilles' heel of these businesses. Therefore the enhancement of access to private equity capital for SME becomes an increasingly pressing issue with far-reaching implications for the German economy at large.

6.3 Limitations

This study identified critical success factors in the realization of private equity backed succession buyouts in German family businesses. Moreover, the systematic specification of dimensions impacting on success is useful in heightening understanding pertaining to this relatively unexplored form of succession among family businesses. However, the research necessarily implies a number of limitations.

(1) Limited generalizability: It is believed that value in family business- and private equity related research is not solely procurable by the employment of quantitative measures but also by broad qualitative inquiry used to better understand the entirety of factors affecting success in private equity backed succession buyouts. In-depth interview research accommodates the complex and multi-dimensional nature of private equity backed succession buyouts and ideally fits the explorative character of this research project. However, the qualitative research methodology employed captures nuances and a great number of details at the expense of generalizability of research results.

(2) Critical success factors change over time: As has become clear in earlier chapters, critical success factors are not a standard set of measures. They are the particular areas of major importance at a particular point in time and change as preferences of involved or exogenous environmental conditions change or as particular problems or opportunities arise. In that way, due to the financial crisis 2008/2009 the specification and weight of success factors attributable to the economic environment appear to have shifted considerably in recent months.

(3) Myopic perspective: This research focused on factors affecting the realization of private equity backed succession buyouts in German family businesses. In this study the closure of the buyout transaction was the central criterion to benchmark success. However, it was shown that success necessarily is a relative parameter and that several different criteria to measure success against are conceivable. For example, it is sensible to measure success against the achievement of objectives of the involved over time. However, since the author decided to focus this study's investigation on the succession process itself, a longitudinal study of factors impacting on business respectively investment success ex post seemed inadequate.

(4) Narrow perspective: The exploitation of multiple interviews with representatives from all four groups principally involved in private equity backed succession buyouts in family businesses has minimized the introduction of error into the results generated. However, this data triangulation approach only accounted for interview accounts from members of the most obvious groups involved in the process. Other perspectives (such as perspectives of other stakeholders) were not included.

(5) German literature: The enfolded literature comprises primarily German literature. The reason being that this study focused on private equity backed succession buyouts in *German* family businesses; thus the amplified use of German literature seems practicable. However, much of the literature dealing with pri-

vate equity related issues tends to be published in Anglo-American journals. This literature has not been focus of this study.

6.4 Suggestions for future research

The study's findings open up room for future research. In particular this holds true with regard to testing the strength of identified success factors conducive to realizing private equity backed succession buyouts quantitatively. A flux of additional research foci is conceivable. Future research in the following topical areas appears to be of immediate value:

(1) Quantitative validation of findings presented in this study: This could be achieved by administering a survey to a preferably large group of individuals from groups already focused on in this study. A research project making use of quantitative (standardized) research methods could then directly build on and test for success factors identified in the present study.

(2) Longitudinal study of private equity backed succession buyouts: In the search for factors affecting the realization of private equity backed succession buyouts in German family businesses the long-term implications of such succession routes were largely factored out. Despite methodological challenges in realizing such a study it would be desirable to have such longitudinal findings.

(3) Comparative study of private equity backed succession buyouts: It was highlighted in this study that the private equity investment activity in Germany is below the European average and considerably behind the activity of the United States. In consideration of this divergence the question arises to what degree the success factors identified in this study are transferable to other countries.

(4) Exclusive focus on behavioral aspects of non-family succession routes: It appears needful to further research behavioral patterns and motivational aspects of family business owners that opt for non-family succession routes regardless of whether or not intergenerational succession is sensibly realizable. This would also help to better understand the circumstances under which private equity backed succession buyouts are realized.

In general terms, more research concerning non-family succession alternatives is desirable. Considering the depreciating number of intra-family successions and the relevance of sustainable succession solutions for the economy at large the amount of research dedicated to non-family succession routes appears to be surprisingly remote.

6.5 Outlook

Despite a flux of factors opposing transaction success the number of private equity backed succession buyouts in German family businesses is likely to increase in the long-term. Foremost, this trend should be carried by a sustained inflow of capital into the private equity market in the long-term and a strengthened purchasing power of private equity investment companies. Two interview partners in this study in particular argued that the national and international private equity market is destined to structurally grow markedly in the next 10 to 20 years. At the same time, for different reasons discussed earlier in this study, the number of family businesses opting for non-family succession alternatives by trend is rising. In addition, in particular buyout managers targeting to succeed existing owners in medium- and large-sized family businesses continue to depend on external equity investors in the buyout process.

Due to the remarkable inflow of capital into the private equity asset class over recent years and a steady increase in the successful completion of private equity sponsored transactions a heightened public awareness of the activity of private equity investment companies is observable. In addition, increasingly factual media coverage of the investment activity of private equity investment companies has effected a demystification of the mechanisms that lie at the heart of the private equity investment process. These are signs suggesting a gradual reduction of prevailing misconceptions in context of institutional private equity financings.

On the side of family business owners a cutback of prejudices towards institutional private equity appears expedient since banks are increasingly withdrawing from financing German SME due to risk-reward considerations and increased administrative burdens (Basel II). Supported by these circumstances the general acceptance among German SME to work with private equity investment companies is likely to grow in the longer-term.

However, in face of the 2008/2009 financial market crisis the debt financing environment in Germany has turned increasingly difficult. This not only affects medium-sized family businesses and private equity investment companies in general but also private equity backed succession buyouts in particular. At this point it becomes apparent that a pronounced shifting of those factors constituting the framework conditions to a private equity backed succession buyout immediately impact on the likelihood of realizing such a transaction. However, it must be assumed that the profound shifting of the economic environment only is of temporary nature and that financial markets - including the market for private equity financings - continue to recover to full stability in due course.

Regardless of the evolution of the 2008/2009 financial market crisis a private equity backed succession buyout is likely to remain a succession route appealing to a minority of family business owners only. However, this study should have shown that institutional private equity investors are able to contribute positively to the realization of succession in medium-sized German family businesses in a pertinent number of cases. In turn the author hopes that this study contributes to a more differentiated and objective treatment of private equity backed succession buyouts in medium-sized German family businesses.

References

Achleitner A.-K., C. H. Fingerle (2003) *Unternehmenswertsteigerung durch Management Buyout*. EF Working Paper Series No. 01-03. München.

Achleitner A.-K., A. Poech (2004). *Familienunternehmen und Private Equity: Die psychologischen Bruchstellen.* Apax Partners (Eds.). München.

Achleitner A.-K., S. C. Schraml, O. Klöckner (2008a) *Finanzierung von Familienunternehmen: Wie professionell ist die Unternehmensfinanzierung tatsächlich?* Droege & Comp., AlphaZirkel (Eds.). München.

Achleitner A.-K. S. C. Schraml, F. Tappeiner (2008b) *Private Equity in Familienunternehmen: Erfahrungen mit Minderheitsbeteiligungen.* Stiftung Familienunternehmen (Eds.). München.

Albach H., W. Freund (1989) *Generationswechsel und Unternehmenskontinuität – Chancen, Risiken, Maßnahmen.* Gütersloh.

Albach H., D. Köster (1997) *Risikokapital in Deutschland.* Discussion Paper FS IV 97-17, Wissenschaftszentrum Berlin. Berlin.

Albach H. W. (1991) *Die Bedeutung neuer Entwicklungen in der Wettbewerbstheorie für die strategische Unternehmensführung.* In Ordelheide D. et al. (Eds.) Betriebswirtschaftslehre und ökonomische Theorie: 255-272. Stuttgart.

Ansoff I., E. McDonnell (1990) *Implanting Strategic Management.* New York.

Arnold W. (1989) *Finanzierungsziele: Anforderungen mittelständischer Unternehmungen an Beteiligungskapital.* Frankfurt/Main.

Atteslander P. (2003) *Methoden der Sozialforschung.* 10. Auflage. Berlin.

Axelrod R. (1980) *Effective choice in the prisoner's dilemma.* Journal of Conflict Resolution. Vol. 24: 3-25.

Bader H. (1996) *Private Equity als Anlagekategorie: Theorie, Praxis und Portfoliomanagement für institutionelle Investoren.* Dissertation, St. Gallen.

Ballwieser W., H. Schmid (1990) *Charakteristika und Problembereiche von Management Buy-Outs.* WISU. Vol. 19(5/6): 299-305 und 358-363.

Baumüller K. (1988) *Unternehmenshandel – Handel in Unternehmen und Beteiligungen.* Frankfurt/Main.

Bea F. X., J. Haas (1995) *Strategisches Management.* Stuttgart.

Bechtle C. (1983) *Die Sicherung der Führungsnachfolge in der Familienunternehmung.* Frankfurt/Main.

Benston G. J., C. W. Smith (1976) *The transaction cost approach to the theory of financial intermediation.* Journal of Finance, Vol. 31: 215-231.

Bergamin S. (1995) *Der Fremdverkauf einer Familienunternehmung im Nachfolgeprozess: Motive, Vorgehenskonzept, externe Unterstützung.* Dissertation, St. Gallen.

Bernet B., C. L. Denk (2000) *Finanzierungsmodelle für KMU*. Bern.

Bitzer K. (1977) *Der mittelständische Unternehmer – einige betriebssoziologische Aspekte*. Dissertation, Berlin.

Bock M. (1992) *Das halbstrukturierte-leitfadenorientierte Tiefeninterview: Theorie und Praxis der Methode am Beispiel von Paarinterviews*. In Hoffmeyer-Zlotnik J. H. P. (Ed.): Analyse verbaler Daten - Über den Umgang mit qualitativen Daten: 91-109. Opladen.

Bontrop H. J. (1999) *Personalwirtschaftliche Überlegungen zur Definition eines mittelständischen Unternehmens*. Betrieb und Wirtschaft (BuW), 53. Jahrgang, Heft 3/1999: 103-119.

Bovaird C. (1990) *Introduction to Venture Capital Finance*. London.

Bullen C. (1981) *A Primer on Critical Success Factors*. No. 1220-81: Sloan Working Paper. Cambridge MA.

Bussiek J. (1996) *Anwendungsorientierte Betriebswirtschaftslehre für Klein- und Mittelunternehmen.* München.

Buttignon F., M. Vedovato, P. Bortuluzzi, A. Gervasoni, R. Del Giudice, F. Bollazzi, C. Soppelsa (2004) *Family Business Investor Buyouts: The Italian Case.* Working Paper, University of Padua. Padua.

Bundesverband deutscher Kapitalbeteiligungsgesellschaften / BVK (Ed.) (2007a) *BVK Statistik – Das Jahr 2006 in Zahlen*. Berlin, 20.02.2007. Retrieved 10.11.2007 from http://www.bvk-ev.de/media/file/110.BVK_Jahresstatistik_2006_200207.pdf

Bundesverband deutscher Kapitalbeteiligungsgesellschaften / BVK (Ed.) (2007b) *Detaillierte Untersuchung der Investitionen und Exits bei Buyout Transaktionen im Rahmen der BVK-Gesamtstatistik*. Berlin, 22.03.2006. Retrieved 10.11.2007 from http://www.bvk-ev.de/media/file/113.BVK_Teilstatistik_Buy-outs2006_220307.pdf

Cable D., S. Shane (1997) *A prisoner's dilemma approach to entrepreneur-venture capitalist relationships*. Academy of Management Review. Vol. 1(22): 142-176.

Cropley A. J. (2002) *Qualitative Forschungsmethoden: eine praxisnahe Einführung*. Eschborn.

Daschmann H.-A. (1994) *Erfolgsfaktoren mittelständischer Unternehmen*. Stuttgart.

DeAngelo H., L. DeAngelo, E. M. Rice (1984) *Going Private: The Effect of Change in Corporate Ownership Structure.* Midland Corporate Finance Journal. Vol 2: 35-43.

Deutscher Sparkassen und Giroverband (Ed.) (2004a) *Diagnose Mittelstand 2004 – Reformprozess verbreitern: Klare Signale und mehr Freiräume für den Mittelstand.* Berlin. Retrieved 01.02.2008 from http://www.smittelstand.de/diagnose_mittelstand_2004.pdf

Deutscher Sparkassen und Giroverband (Ed.) (2004b) *Diagnose Mittelstand 2004 – Statistischer Anhang.* Berlin. Retrieved 01.02.2008 from http://www.smittelstand.de/diagnose_tabellenanhang_neu.pdf

DeRidder P. (1990) *Finanzierung von Buyouts.* In Bank, C. (Ed.): Management Buy-out: 59-65. Frankfurt/Main.

Dresdner Bank/Impulse (Ed.) (2000) *mind finance – Mittelstand in Deutschland.* Köln.

Dresdner Bank/Impulse (Ed.) (2002) *mind 02 – Mittelstand in Deutschland.* Köln. Retrieved 10.10.2007 from http://www.ifm-bonn.org/assets/documents/Mind-02.pdf

European Commission (Ed.) (2002) *Abschlußbericht der Sachverständigengruppe zur Übertragung von kleinen und mittleren Unternehmen.* Brüssel. Retrieved 15.11.2007 from http://ec.europa.eu/enterprise/entrepreneurship/support_measures/transfer_business/transfer_com_02/final_report_de.pdf

European Commission (Ed.) (2003) *Empfehlung der Europäischen Kommission vom 06/05/2003 betreffend die Definition der Kleinstunternehmen sowie der kleinen und mittleren Unternehmen.* Brüssel, 2003. Retrieved 15.11.2007 from http://ec.europa.eu/enterprise/enterprise_policy/sme_definition/sme_user_guide_de.pdf

European Commission (Ed.) (2006) *Märkte für Unternehmensübertragungen – Förderung transparenter Marktplätze für Unternehmensübertragungen in Europa.* Brüssel, 2006. Retrieved 31.03.2008 from http://www.pedz.uni-mannheim.de/daten/edz-h/gdb/03/transfer_markets_de.pdf

European Private Equity and Venture Capital Association / EVCA (Ed.) (2008) *EVCA Annual Survey of Pan-European Private Equity & Venture Capital Activity 2007.* Retrieved 28.06.08 from http://www.evca.eu

European Private Equity and Venture Capital Association / EVCA (Ed.) (2005) *Private Equity and Generational Change: The Contribution of Private Equity to the Succession of Family Businesses in Europe.* Zaventem.

European Private Equity and Venture Capital Association / EVCA (Ed.) (2003) *Benchmark Paper: Benchmarking European Tax & Legal Environments.* Zaventem.

FAZ-Institut (Ed.) (2003) *FAZ-Institut für Management-, Markt- und Medieninformationen: MBO als Nachfolgelösung.* Frankfurt/Main. Retrieved 14.01.2008 from http://www.deutsche-beteiligung.de/files/mbo_als_nachfolgelosung.pdf

Fama E. F., M. C. Jensen (1983) *Agency problems and residual claims.* Journal of Law and Economics. Vol. 26: 327-350.

Felden B, A. Klaus (2003) *Unternehmensnachfolge.* Stuttgart.

Fenn G. W., N. Liang, S. Prowse (1995) *The Economics of the Private Equity Market. The Board of Govenors of the Federal Reserve System.* Working Paper 168. Retrieved 10.11.2007 from http:// econpapers.repec.org/ paper/fipfedgss/168.htm

Forst M. (1992) *Management Buy-out und Buy-in als Form der Übernahme mittelständischer Unternehmen.* Stuttgart.

Frank M. A. (2002) *Die "kleine" AG als Organisationsform für die Nachfolge in Familienunternehmen.* Baden-Baden.

Freund W., G. Kayser, E. Schroer (1995) *Generationswechsel im Mittelstand: Unternehmensübertragungen und –übernahmen 1995 bis 2000.* Materialien des Instituts für Mittelstandsfroschung, Nr. 109. Bonn.

Freund W. (2000) *Familieninterne Unternehmensnachfolge, Erfolgs- und Risikofaktoren.* Wiesbaden.

Frommann H. (2003) Geleitwort. In Jugel S. (Ed.) *Private Equity Investments*: V-X. Wiesbaden.

Fudenberg D., J. Tirole (1991) *Game Theory.* Cambridge MA.

Gälweiler A. (1990) *Strategische Unternehmensführung*. Frankfurt/Main.

Gerke W., F. Phillip (1985) *Finanzierung*. Stuttgart.

Gersik K., J. Davis, M. M. Hampton, I. Landsberg (1997) *Generation to Generation: Life Cycles of the Family Business*. Boston.

Gephart R. (2004) *From the editors: Qualitative Research and the Academy of Management Journal*. Academy of Management Journal. Vol. 8: 454-462.

Gladstone D. (1988) *Venture Capital Handbook*. Englewood Cliffs.

Glaser B., A. Strauss (1967) *The Discovery of Grounded Theory: Strategies for qualitative research*. New York.

Grochla E., M. Puhlmann, M. Vahle (1984) *Die Entlastung mittelständischer Unternehmer durch organisatorische Maßnahmen: Ergebnisse aus einer Befragung von 79 mittelständischen Führungskräften.* Zeitschrift für betriebswirtschaftliche Forschung. Vol. 36(5): 395-411.

Günterberg B., H.-J. Wolter (2002) *Unternehmensgrößenstatistik 2001/2002: Daten und Fakten, Nr. 157*. Institut für Mittelstandsforschung. Bonn.

Gutenberg E. (1976) *Grundlagen der Betriebswirtschaftslehre*, Band II, Der Absatz. Berlin.

Hack A. (2005) *Startuperfolg und die Wahl von Risikokapitalgebern – Ökonomische Analyse mit empirischer Validierung für den deutschen Markt.* Dissertation, Koblenz.

Hamel G. (1991) *Competing for competence and interpartner learning within international strategic alliances.* Strategic Management Journal, Vol. 12: 83-103.

Hanney J. (1986) *The management buy-out – an offer you can't refuse.* Omega, Vol. 14: 119-134.

Häupler J. (2001) *Virtuelle Marktplätze für Private Equity.* Dissertation, Wien.

Hellwig M. (1991) *Banking, financial intermediation and corporate finance.* In Giovannini A., C. Mayer (Eds.) European Financial Integration: 35-63. Cambridge.

Hennerkes B.H. (1998) *Familienunternehmen sichern und optimieren.* Stuttgart.

Hennerkes B.-H, C. Pleister (Eds.) (1999) *Erfolgsmodell Mittelstand – 12 Unternehmer geben Einblicke in ihr Denken und Handeln.* Wiesbaden.

Hering T., M. Olbrich (2003) *Unternehmensnachfolge.* München/Wien.

Hoffmann P., R. Ramke (1990) *Management Buy-Out in der Bundesrepublik Deutschland – Anspruch, Realität und Perspektiven.* Münster.

Hoffmann-Hampe H. (1994) *Der Beitrag des Management-Buyout bei der Transformation staatlicher Planwirtschaften: Ein deutsch-polnischer Vergleich.* Dissertation, Gdansk.

Holthausen R. W, D. F. Larcker (1996) *The Financial Performance of Reverse Leveraged Buyouts.* Journal of Financial Economics. Vol. 42(3): 293.

Holzapfel H. J., R. Pöllath (2000) *Unternehmenskauf in Recht und Praxis – Rechtliche und steuerliche Aspekte.* Köln.

Homans G. C. (1950) *The Human Group.* New York.

Hommel U., H. Schneider (2003) *Financing the German Mittelstand.* EIB Papers. Vol 8(2): 53-90.

Howorth C. P., P. Westhead, M. Wright (2004) *Information Asymmetry in Management Buyouts of Family Firms.* Journal of Business Venturing, Vol. 19(4): 509-534.

Huber H. G., H. Sterr-Kölln (2006) *Nachfolge in Familienunternehmen.* Stuttgart.

Huydts H. J. (1992) *Management Buyout als strategische Option zur Regelung der Nachfolge in mittelgroßen Familienunternehmen – Erfolgsfaktoren und Gestaltungsvarianten.* Dissertation, St. Gallen.

Institut für Mittelstandsforschung Bonn / IfM Bonn (Ed.) (2005) *Stabwechsel – die schwierige Suche nach dem richtigen Nachfolger.* Präsentation 3. Expertenforum Mittelstand am 14.04.2005 in München. Retrieved 04.03.2007 from http://www.ifm-bonn.org

Institut für Mittelstandsforschung Bonn / IfM Bonn (Ed.) (2007a) *Die volkswirtschaftliche Bedeutung der Familienunternehmen.* IfM Bonn, Stiftung Familienunternehmen (Eds.). Bonn.

Institut für Mittelstandsforschung Bonn / IfM Bonn (Ed.) (2007b) *Aktualisierte Statistik der Unternehmensnachfolgen auf Grundlage der im Jahrbuch zur Mittelstandsforschung Heft 1/2004 veröffentlichten Untersuchung*. Retrieved 05.12.2007 from http://www.ifm-bonn.org

Institut für Mittelstandsforschung Bonn /IfM Bonn (Ed.) (2007c) *Mittelstand – Definitionen und Schüsselzahlen*. Bonn. Retrieved 13.11.2007 from http://www.ifm-bonn.org

Institut für Mittelstandsforschung Mannheim / IfM Mannheim (Ed.) (2003) *Generationswechsel in Baden-Württemberg – Zum richtigen Zeitpunkt den richtigen Nachfolger ins Spiel bringen*. IfM Mannheim, DZ Bank (Eds.). Mannheim.

Jakoby S. (2000) *Erfolgsfaktoren von Management Buyout in Deutschland: eine empirische Untersuchung*. Lohmar/Köln.

Jansen A. (1986) *Desinvestitionen – Ursachen, Probleme und Gestaltungsmöglichkeiten*. Dissertation, Frankfurt/Main.

Jensen M. C., W. H. Meckling (1976) *Theory of the firm: Managerial behavior, agency costs, and ownership structure*. Journal of Financial Economics Vol. 3(4): 305-360.

Jost P. J. (2000) *Organisation und Koordination*. Eine Ökonomische Einführung. Wiesbaden.

Jost P. J. (2001) *Der Transaktionskostenansatz im Unternehmenskontext*. In Jost (Ed.). Der Transaktionskostenansatz in der Betriebswirtschaftslehre: 9-34. Stuttgart.

Kaplan S. N., J. C. Stein (1993) *The Evolution of Buyout Pricing and Financial Structure in the 1980s*. Journal of Applied Corporate Finance, Vol 6: 72-88.

Kaufmann F., L. Kokalj (1996) *Risikokapitalmärkte für mittelständische Unternehmen*. Schriften zur Mittelstandsforschung 68. Stuttgart.

Kell T. (2005) *Management Due Diligence und Management-Entwicklung als Hebel zur Wertsteigerung*. In Berens W., H. U. Brauner, J. Frodermann (Eds.): Unternehmensentwicklung mit Finanzinvestoren: 149-160. Stuttgart.

Kennedy M. M. (1979) *Generalizing from single case studies*. Evaluation Quarterly Vol. 3(4): 661-678.

Kern E. (1990) *Der Interaktionsansatz im Investitionsgütermarketing – eine konfirmatorische Analyse*. Berlin.

KfW Bankengruppe (Ed.) (2006) *Mittelstandsmonitor: Jährlicher Bericht zu Konjunktur- und Strukturfragen kleiner und mittlerer Betriebe*. Frankfurt/Main.

Kitching J. (1989) *Early Returns on LBOs.* Harvard Business Review, Vol. 6: 74-81.

Klein S. B. (2000) *Familienunternehmen; theoretische und empirische Grundlagen.* Wiesbaden.

Koch W., J. Wegmann (2002) *Praktiker-Handbuch Due Diligence - Analyse mittelständischer Unternehmen.* Stuttgart.

Kokalj L. (1994) *Die wirtschaftliche Entwicklung von MBO-Unternehmen in den neuen Bundesländern: Eine Längsschnittuntersuchung.* Bonn.

Krimphove D., D. Tytko (2003) *Der Begriff „mittelständische Unternehmen" in betriebswirtschaftlicher und juristischer Diskussion.* In Schmeisser W., D. Krimphove, K. Nathusius (Eds.): Handbuch Unternehmensnachfolge: 3-13. Stuttgart.

Kussmaul H. (1983) *Unternehmerkinder: Ihre zivil- und steuerrechtliche Berücksichtigung in personenbezogenen, mittelständischen Familienunternehmen.* Köln.

Kvale S. (2007) *Doing Interviews.* London.

Le Mar B. (2001) *Generations- und Führungswechsel in Familienunternehmen.* Heidelberg.

Leopold G., H. Frommann, T. Kühr (2003) *Private Equity – Venture Capital: Eigenkapital für innovative Unternehmer*, 2. Auflage. München.

Lew M. I., E. A. Kolodzeij (1993) *Compensation in a family-owned business.* Human Resources Professional, Vol. 5(3): 55-75.

Linnemann C. (2007) *Deutscher Mittelstand vom Aussterben bedroht? Unternehmensnachfolge im Fokus.* Deutsche Bank Research (Eds.). Frankfurt. Retrieved 30.09.2007 from http://www.dbresearch.com

Lorenz T. (1989) *Venture Capital Today.* New York.

Luhmann N. (2004) *Einführung in die Systemtheorie*, 2. Auflage. Heidelberg.

Luippold T. (1991) *Management Buyouts – Evaluation ihrer Einsatzmöglichkeiten in Deutschland.* Dissertation, St. Gallen.

Lütjen G. (1992) *Management Buy-Out. Firmenübernahmen durch Management und Belegschaft.* Wiesbaden.

Matthews R. C. O. (1986) *The Economics of Institutions and the Source of Growth.* The Economic Journal, Vol. 96: 903-918.

Mestwerdt C. (1998) *Management-auf-Zeit in kleinen und mittleren Unternehmen (KMU).* Dissertation, St. Gallen.

Milgrom P., J. Roberts (1992) *Economics, Organization and Management.* Englewood Cliffs.

Mittendorfer R. (2001) *Finanzierungsmodelle von Leveraged Buyout.* In W. Stadler (Ed.): Venture Capital und Private Equity – Erfolgreich wachsen mit Beteiligungskapital: 141-184. Köln.

Morck R. (1996) *On the economics of concentrated ownership.* Canadian Business Law Journal, Vol. 26: 63-75.
Mummendey A. (1985) *Verhalten zwischen sozialen Gruppen: Die Theorie der sozialen Identität.* In Frey D., M. Irle (Eds.): Theorien der Sozialpsychologie, Bd. II: Gruppen- und Lerntheorien: 185-216. Bern.

Nathusius K. (2003) *Die Finanzierungsnachfolge mit Beteiligungskapital – Eine Betrachtung aus Sicht von Venture Capital Gesellschaften.* In Schmeisser W., D. Krimphove, K. Nathusius (Eds.): Handbuch Unternehmensnachfolge: 360-390. Stuttgart.
Nathusius K., E. Bohm (2003) *Management Buy-In Finanzierung – Grundsätze und Beispiele von Unternehmensnachfolgen.* In Schmeisser et al. (Eds.): Handbuch Unternehmensnachfolge: 431-445. Stuttgart.

Olbrich M. (2003) *Unternehmensnachfolge und Unternehmensgründung – eine terminologische Abgrenzung.* In Walterscheid K. (Ed.): Entrepreneurship in Forschung und Lehre – Festschrift für Klaus Anderseck: 133-145. Frankfurt/Main.

Perridon L., M. Steiner (1993) *Finanzwirtschaft der Unternehmung.* München.
Pfohl H. C. (1997) *Abgrenzung der Klein- und Mittelbetriebe von Großbetrieben.* In Pfohl H. C. (Ed.): Betriebswirtschaftslehre der Mittel- und Kleinbetriebe – Größenspezifische Probleme und Möglichkeiten zu Ihrer Lösung, 3. Auflage: 1-25. Berlin.
Picot A. (1982) *Transaktionskostenansatz in der Organisationstheorie: Stand der Diskussion und Aussagewert.* Betriebswirtschaft, Vol. 42: 267-284.
Pichotta A. (1990) *Die Prüfung der Beteiligungswürdigkeit von innovativen Unternehmungen durch Venture Capital–Gesellschaften.* Bergisch-Gladbach.
Plagge A. (2006) *Public policy for venture capital: A comparison of the United States and Germany.* Dissertation, Wiesbaden.
Prätsch J., U. Schikorra, E. Ludwig (2007) *Finanzmanagement.* Berlin.

Reimers N. (2004) *Private Equity für Familienunternehmen.* Wiesbaden.
Riedel H. (2000) *Unternehmensnachfolge regeln*, 3. Auflage. Wiesbaden.
Rosenbauer C. (1994) *Strategische Erfolgsfaktoren des Familienunternehmens im Rahmen seines Lebenszyklus.* Dissertation, St. Gallen.

Sachverständigenrat (Ed.) (2005) *Kapitalmarkt und Finanzintermediäre: Unternehmensfinanzierung im Wandel, Jahresgutachten 2005/2006.* Wiesbaden. Retrieved 03.03.2007 from http://www.sachverstaendigenrat-wirtschaft.de/download/gutachten/ga05_vii.pdf

Schäfer D., A. Fisher (2008) *Die Bedeutung von Buy-Outs/Ins für unternehmerische Effizienz, Effektivität und Corporate Governance*. DIW/BVK (Eds.). Berlin.

Schefczyk M. (2006) *Finanzieren mit Venture Capital und Private Equity*. Stuttgart.

Schefczyk M. (2003) *Finanzieren mit Venture Capital*. In Krimphove D., D. Tytko (Eds.): Praktiker-Handbuch Unternehmensfinanzierung: 95-117. Stuttgart.

Schefczyk M. (2000) *Finanzieren mit Venture Capital. Grundlagen für Investoren, Finanzintermediäre, Unternehmer und Wissenschaftler*. Stuttgart.

Scherer S., K. Hermut, M. Blanc, T. Groth, R. Wimmer (2005) *Familienunternehmen. Erfolgsstrategien zur Unternehmenssicherung*. Frankfurt.

Schließmann C. P., A. Fandrich (2001) *Unternehmer-Nachfolge*. Neuwied.

Schmid H. (1994) *Leveraged management buy-out: Begriff, Gestaltungen, optimale Kapitalstruktur und ökonomische Bewertung*. Dissertation, Frankfurt/Main.

Schmidt S. L. (2003) *Kombination qualitativer und quantitativer empirischer Forschungsmethode: Analyse von Strategieprozessen*. In Schwaiger M., D. Harhoff (Eds.): Empirie und Betriebswirtschaft – Entwicklungen und Perspektiven: 139-153. Stuttgart.

Schwaninger M. (1989) *Integrale Unternehmensplanung*. Frankfurt/Main.

Schröer E., W. Freund (1999) *Neue Entwicklungen auf dem Markt für Übertragungen mittelständischer Unternehmen*. IfM Materialien Nr. 136. Bonn.

Schröer S., G. Kayser (2006) *Beratungsbedarf und Beratungspraxis bei Unternehmensnachfolgen*. In Institut für Mittelstandsforschung Bonn (Ed.): Jahrbuch zur Mittelstandsforschung 1/2006, Schriften zur Mittelstandsforschung Nr. 112 NF: 1-44. Wiesbaden.

Sewing P. (1992) *Kauf von kleinen und mittleren Unternehmen durch aktive Privatinvestoren – Marktfaktoren in Deutschland, Unternehmensbewertung und Vermögenssteigerungseffekte*. Dissertation, Bamberg.

Sharma P., P. G. Irving (2005) *Four Bases of Family Business Successor Commitment: Antecedents and Consequences*. Entrepreneurship Theory and Practice, Vol. 29(1): 13-33.

Singh H. (1990) *Management Buyouts: Distinguishing Characteristics and Operating Changes Prior to Public Offering*. Strategic Management Journal. Vol 11: 111-129.

Spielmann U. (1994) *Der Generationswechsel in mittelständischen Unternehmungen bei Gründern und Nachfolgern*. Dissertation, St. Gallen.

Spies B.-G., U. Thess (2005) *Management Audit*. In Berens W., H. U. Brauner, J. Frodermann (Eds.): Unternehmensentwicklung mit Finanzinvestoren: 161-170. Stuttgart.

Stephan P. (2002) *Nachfolge in mittelständischen Familienunternehmen: Handlungsempfehlungen aus Sicht der Unternehmensführung*. Wiesbaden.

Stracke M. (2005) *Nachfolge von Familienfremden Dritten*. In Sudhoff H. (Ed.): Familienunternehmen. München.

Schwetje G., S. Vaseghi (2007) *The Business Plan – How to Win Your Investor's Confidence*. Berlin.

Then Bergh F. (1998) *Leveraged Management Buyout: Konzept und agencytheoretische Analyse*. Dissertation, Düsseldorf.

Thompson R. S. (1988) *Management buyouts: A review of trends*. In De Caires B., M. Wright (Eds.): Management Buyouts. London.

Tietzel M. (1981) *Die Ökonomie der Property-Rights: Ein Überblick*. Zeitschrift für Wirtschaftspolitik, Vol 30: 207-243.

Tykvova T. (2005) *Finanzierung, Börsengang und Performance mit unterschiedlichen Venture-Capital-Gebern*. ZEW Wirtschaftsanalyzen. Frankfurt/Main.

Vest P. (1995) *Der Verkauf von Konzernunternehmen durch Management Buyout*. Dissertation, Wiesbaden.

Von Boxberg F. (1991) *Das Management Buy-out Konzept: Eine Möglichkeit zur Herauslösung krisenhafter GmbH-Tochterunternehmen*. Hamburg.

Weber-Rey D. (2001) *Private Equity Transaktionen*. In Semler J., R. Vollhard (Eds.): Arbeitshandbuch für Unternehmensübernahmen: 591-655. München.

Weinländer H. (1998) *Unternehmensnachfolge*. München.

Weißenberger B. E. (1997) *Die Informationsbeziehung zwischen Management und Rechnungswesen. Analyse institutionaler Koordination*. Wiesbaden.

Wernerfeld B. (1984) *A Resource-based view of the Firm*. Strategic Management Journal. Vol. 5(2): 171-181.

Wiedmann T. (2002) *Unternehmensnachfolge in einem krisenbedrohten Familienunternehmen mit Berücksichtigung persönlicher Ansprüche der Unternehmer*. Dissertation, St. Gallen.

Williamson O. E. (1985) *The Economic Institutions of Capitalism: Firms, Markets, Relational Contracting*. New York.

Wippenbeck A. (1984) *Einkünftezurechnung bei Familienunternehmen*. Neuried.

Wright M., J. Coyne (1985) *Management Buyouts*. Bechenham.

Wright M., K. Robbie (1998) *Venture Capital and Private Equity: A Review and Synthesis*. Journal of Business Finance & Accounting. Vol. 25: 521-570.

Yin R. K. (1994) *Case study research: design and methods*. Thousand Oaks CA.

Index of figures and tables

Abbreviations

BIMBO	buyin management buyout
BVK	Bundesverband deutscher Kapitalbeteiligungsgesellschaften
EVCA	European Private Equity and Venture Capital Association
et al.	et alii
et sq.	et sequens
et sqq.	et sequentes
HGB	Handelsgesetzbuch
IfM	Institut für Mittelstandsforschung
IRR	internal rate of return
IPO	initial public offering
LBO	leveraged buyout
LOI	letter of intent
m	million
M&A	mergers & acquisitions
MBO	management buyout
MBI	management buyin
PE	private equity
SME	small and medium-sized enterprises
VAT	value added tax

Peter Lang · Internationaler Verlag der Wissenschaften

Donika Lilova

Bulgaria as a Target for Foreign Direct Investment

Frankfurt am Main, Berlin, Bern, Bruxelles, New York, Oxford, Wien, 2009.
XVI, 84 pp., 4 fig., num. tab.
European University Studies: Series 5, Economics and Management. Vol. 3335
ISBN 978-3-631-59361-5 · pb. € 19.80*

The book aims at providing an objective investment picture of Bulgaria. It is based on empirical criteria concerning the attractiveness of Bulgaria as a location for FDI. Additional task of the Thesis is the comparison of Bulgaria's political, macroeconomic and legal business environment, the production conditions and market opportunities with two successful Central European countries and with the neighbouring Romania. Part of the analysis included a comprehensive online survey with leading European entrepreneurs and investors. The author presents a well-weighted picture of the positive and negative factors of Bulgaria as a target for Foreign Direct Investment.

Contents: Foreign Direct Investment · Empirical criteria for choosing the right location for FDI · The Republic of Bulgaria · Foreign Direct Investment in Bulgaria · Factors determining the attractiveness for FDI · Empirical evaluation of Bulgaria as a target for FDI